This book is dedicated to my grandchildren:

Jack, Gracie, A.J., Brooklyn, Carson,

and our sweet Ellie in Heaven,

May you always walk with God and follow His Holy Will!

In Gratitude

First, I want to give thanks and praise to our Lord and God. He has blessed me in ways that surprise and amaze me every day. God guided me to share my endless love for Him and my faith journey. My God is an awesome God!

Second, I want to thank the many people who have encouraged me to write a second faith journey book. Many beautiful people have blessed me with their support, encouragement, and suggestions.

Special thanks to Melanie Florio and Tonya McDonald, who told me I had to write this book.

Special thanks to my cousins Deb Bourque and Beth Kelly for their support and encouragement.

A very special thank you to Melanie Florio, Anna Mae Paladina, Meg Nichol, and Diane Blizard, who proofread my book and gave me suggestions and edits.

Thanks for all the prayers and support from the powerful prayer warriors who pray with me every night, especially Carolyn Wright! You are a blessing to me, and I will be forever grateful for all your help and prayers!

Third, I want to thank Ellen Gable Hrkach, James Hrkach, and Daniel Oviedo. I could not imagine doing book two without your help and expertise. You made it possible for me to cross the goal line and complete this book. May God richly bless you and your careers.

Last but never least, this book would not be possible without the love and support of my husband, John! He is the reason I have such a faith-filled life. John kept his promise to be my life partner and walk with me on our journey to Heaven.

I look forward to spending eternity with him!

Table of Contents

Introduction

After hearing a clear message in Eucharistic Adoration, I wrote my first book, *If Today You Hear His Voice*. Actually, I am unsure if I wrote it as much as the Holy Spirit directed me on what to write! The book took two and a half years to complete and took me on an amazing faith journey. I cover that story in Chapter 1.

Writing this book was not easy. Since my life is not noteworthy or unique, writing a book about my life was the last thing I thought to do. I strongly and sincerely love Jesus Christ and consider myself one of His followers. Hopefully, you are too! So, when I heard Him ask me to write the book, I listened. I love that He willed me to write this book to share my journey, not because it's noteworthy but because it's like everyone's, maybe not in actual experiences but in the same way God directs, guides, comforts, walks, and talks to us. Do you hear the voice of God? I can assure you He talks to you every day if you are open to hearing His voice.

In conversation with one of my parish priests, I was told that I might never get people's responses to my book because it is too personal for them to share their own relationship with God. I would have to accept that my book had impacted them the way God intended. I had peace with what he said and gave all glory to God. When I did that, a funny thing happened: people started sending me cards and letters telling me what the book meant to them! I was touched by the many stories people shared and realized that our lives are similar. We are all on a journey to seek God. The one comment I heard the most was that my book helped people grow in faith. I loved that God used me to help others know Him!

Thank you if you are reading *Harden Not Your Hearts* because you enjoyed my first book. I have written this book thanks to the encouragement and urging of many people. This is my testimony of God's great love and the graces we can all receive if we don't harden our hearts to the voice of God.

Book two continues the faith teachings with Scripture, prayer, and some of my personal stories. My prayer for you, the reader, is that this book will help you grow in faith and will help you to reflect on your faith journey. May you always be open to hearing the voice of God. *"Oh, that today you would hear His voice! Do not harden your hearts."* (Psalm 95:7-8)

May God bless you.

Chapter 1

If Today You Hear His Voice

It took me two and a half years to write my first book *If Today You Hear His Voice.* My journey began in January 2018. I asked Fr. Russell to bless my husband because he was going into the hospital for a heart procedure. After the blessing, Fr. Russell recommended that my husband stay home for the remainder of the time leading up to the hospital stay. Flu season was in high gear, and he didn't want to see John exposed to it. Father recommended that I bring John the Eucharist on Sunday, and he could watch the Mass on TV.

John followed Father's request, so I went alone to Eucharistic Adoration that Friday. It was there that I heard God's voice.

The best way to describe it is I heard the voice through telepathy. The voice was clear and distinct, but only I could hear it. I was asked to write a book. For some, this may have seemed like a simple request. For me, it was anything but simple. Writing is not my strong suit. I have an analytical mind, which makes me good with numbers, facts, and figures. The grammar police have a field day with my writing. I even tried to get out of the request by saying I did not have enough to write. I should have known better. God knows what He is doing, and He filled my mind with so many examples of what He wanted me to write that I was speechless. Still shocked by this revelation, I asked, "*Do you have a title?*" Without hesitation, I heard the words, *"If Today You Hear His Voice."* You could have knocked me over with a feather when I heard this. You can't imagine how I felt. In disbelief, I went home and told my husband. He encouraged me to write down everything that came to me in Adoration, and I did.

To ensure I didn't get distracted from my charge, I kept hearing Psalm 95: *"Oh, that today you would hear His voice! Do not harden your hearts."*(Psalm 95:7-8) It was a constant reminder in my daily readings and emails, and when I heard it at Mass. God kept talking to me through these reminders. There was no doubt in my mind I was supposed to write this book, but it wasn't easy. Most days, I would sit in front of my computer and stare at the blank screen. It wasn't until I realized I needed to do my writing in Eucharistic Adoration facing the Monstrance and in the Real Presence of Christ that I started to write.

I would start my Holy Hour by asking the Lord to guide me in writing and to direct me in His will. I brought a pad of paper to Adoration and placed my pen in my hand to write. My pen went so fast that I was afraid I would not be able to decipher the words. My husband looked at me in disbelief as he watched the pen move with incredible speed. All he could say was, *"Wow!"*

I replied that it wasn't me writing!

I knew I needed to find an illustrator to draw my book cover. Since I had no idea where to start looking for one, I decided to advertise on Craig's List. I knew a good illustrator could cost between $250 and $1000 for a book cover, but I'm not wealthy. I only offered $100. I was amazed at how many answered the ad, although one did complain that my price was too low. I chose the top three artists and asked for a sample of their work. The one I was drawn to has a unique business name which almost made me *not* consider him. His business is called *"Dead Souls."* I told him my book was the opposite of his name and had reservations about using him. Chris told me that he chose the name when he was much younger. A blank page was like a dead soul he would bring to life. He also shared with me that he was a Christian. So, I asked Chris to draw a sample picture, and I liked what I saw. After negotiating the price to a more realistic amount, I hired him.

At the time, I was discerning what should be on the cover. Still confused over the purpose of writing the book, I decided that, at the very least, it would be a testimony of my faith and life journey for my grandchildren. I wanted the picture to include Christ in the center, surrounded by my grandchildren. My legacy to them would always be to put Christ at the center of their lives.

At the time, my youngest grandchild, Brooklyn, was only two and a half years old. I wanted Christ to hold her hand with His other hand outstretched to welcome others to join Him. My two oldest grandchildren, Gracie and Jack, would be on His left, and my youngest grandchild's brother, AJ, would be next to her on His right. I asked for the girls' outfits to match. Chris also matched the boys in their clothing.

I never mentioned any particular colors or backgrounds. I wanted to allow Chris the freedom to be creative. Whenever I thought of the cover, my mind was filled with the colors yellow and green. So, when the cover was finished, and it was yellow and green, I knew I had the right illustrator!

A professional book editor was picked from a long list of professional editors. After interviewing her, I discovered that she was not Catholic, so I was unsure if she would want to work on my book. In conversation, I learned that her father had been raised Catholic but was now a protestant minister. Since I wanted my book to touch all Catholics and Christians, I knew she would be a good choice. After I finished the first draft of the book, I asked her if it was publish-worthy. Her comment was the only one I wanted to hear. She said the book increased her faith.

I was happy to have my book finished in the summer of 2019, or at least I thought it was finished. I sent the book to several publishers, including Marian Press. My dream was to have it published by Marian Press, located on the property of the Divine Mercy Shrine in Stockbridge, Massachusetts. I had sent them a sample chapter in the summer and was told to expect it would be several months before being contacted.

In October, a group of us from St. Patrick's and Incarnation Church planned a retreat to the Divine Mercy Shrine. I brought a copy of my manuscript to show my travel companions. We rented all but one room in the John Paul II Retreat House and enjoyed a fantastic week thanks to Father Dan Cambra, M.I.C., and Mary Katherine. Mary Katherine gave us a tour of Marian Press and explained that most of their books are published by in-house authors such as Father Michael Gaitley, Father Chris Alar, Vinny Flynn, Father Don Calloway, and of course, they also published St. Faustina's Diary. After hearing this, I realized my book was probably not of the same caliber as these talented writers.

While on our retreat, I received an email from the Marian Press editor asking for a copy of my complete manuscript. They didn't realize I was staying in the John Paul II Retreat House across the street. I walked over with my copy of the manuscript and handed it to them. It was an emotional time for me. God was directing me to the next step. I was excited, happy, nervous, and a little uncertain. I liked most of what I wrote but wasn't completely happy with the final version. Certain parts of the book made me feel uneasy, and there was a disconnect. I couldn't place my finger on what was wrong, but I knew it wasn't finished. Unfortunately,

I just wanted it to be done. It was beginning to feel like a homework assignment that I wanted to turn in and be done with it.

It would take another couple of months before I would hear back from Marian Press, which gave me time to take a break from all my writing. In late December, I received an email from Chris at Marian Press. It was a kind email, even though it was a rejection. Chris could have said thanks, but no thanks, but he did not. Chris did me a tremendous favor. He identified the disconnect and helped me see what I needed to do to correct it. After a few thought-provoking questions, I saw the book in a new light! God used Chris to help me.

I now knew that the book needed to be a conversation with the reader. It wasn't just about my journey but about all our journeys. Although different from yours, my journey is similar in the way we should all see and hear God in everything. This book was to help others see that God walks and talks to all of us!

I decided to be bold enough to ask Chris what I should do next to get published. His comment encouraged me. He felt since I was being led to write the book, the next step would also be given to me at the appropriate time. I am so grateful for his assistance.

He was correct, and many things did happen to guide me toward publication. I met many authors who shared their insights and journeys with me. I learned a lot about the publishing industry in a few short months. I also had the outstanding assistance of my dear friends Anna Mae Paladina, Melanie Florio, Meg Nichol, and Eleanor Nelson. They assisted me with their comments, corrections, and encouragement with my rewrites. My twenty-one-chapter book became twenty-nine chapters, all now in chronological order. I also added prayers, Scripture, and questions to engage the reader. My friends did not hesitate to offer help in proofreading and adding suggestions. It became a team effort!

I was anxious to have the book ready for publication. Two years had quickly passed, and I thought the book was finally finished. I was wrong. The first printing had several errors, including the layout of the book. The table of contents was on the left side, with several spelling errors. It was hard to imagine that we still missed these errors after so many eyes had seen the book, including a paid professional editor. Melanie suggested because we were all so engaged in the story, it was easy to miss small mistakes. I knew I had to stop publication and distribution and correct the errors. Four books were sold before I could do this. If anyone has a book with the table of contents on the left page, I would be happy to send you the corrected version.

There were three things in my book that made me uneasy. It was the feeling I got when I knew the Holy Spirit was trying to warn me. I knew I needed to fix it, but I wasn't sure why or how. Thankfully, God did! He gave me three clear messages. The first one involved a person I spoke about in my book. Although I hadn't seen this person in over fifteen years, God placed her directly in my path and allowed me to have a lengthy conversation with her. I had forgotten how warm, caring, and friendly she was, and I knew I needed to rewrite what I had written. The second message involved a person I wrote about using a negative tone. My memories of her were not all pleasant, but a note slipped out of one of my old photo books when I looked for a picture for my website. This note was a heartwarming and kind message from this person. I don't recall ever seeing this sweet card. I knew I had to change my tone.

The third message I received was an obvious one. I was asked to write my book with love. There could be no negative statements, only the message of love, God's endless love! He then filled me with His love, and I worked on my computer editing my book for three days. After a marathon of thirty hours of rewrites, I received an overwhelming sense that the book was finished. Until then, I never felt that the book would ever be finished. Every time I read it, I made changes. I was never satisfied until now. I knew it was done.

I contacted my editor late on Friday and asked if she would format the final version for publishing. I had asked her several times before to format, so I begged forgiveness and reassured her that I was really finished this time. She sent it back in record time. The publishing company usually took several days to respond, but they accepted the book that evening. I had learned my editor was expecting a child and asked her when her due date was. She told me the delivery would be on Monday. You know everything is right when it works out right down to the last detail. God was with me in every detail!

Let us pray: "*Thank you, Lord, for Your guidance and direction. May I always listen to Your voice, Lord!*"

Chapter 2
Harden Not Your Hearts

"Oh, that today you would hear His voice! Do not harden your hearts." (Psalm 95:7-8)

What does it mean to harden your heart? Did you know this phrase is in the Bible in several places? We hear it in the Old Testament in Psalm 95 and again in the New Testament in Hebrews. *"Therefore, as the holy Spirit says: Oh, that today you would hear His voice! Harden not your hearts as at the rebellion in the day of testing in the desert, where your ancestors tested and tried Me and saw My works for forty years."* (Hebrews 3:7-11)

It is repeated in Hebrews 3:15 and again in Hebrews 4:7. This must be a significant statement to be repeated so many times. The message is vital. It warns against having *"an evil and unfaithful heart, so as to forsake the living God. Encourage yourselves daily while it is still 'today,' so that none of you may grow hardened by the deceit of sin."* (Hebrews 3:13)

We know God is love. *"Anyone who does not love does not know God, because God is love."* (1 John 4:8) He loves each of us. God wants His Word to enter our hearts so that we will know and love Him. If our hearts are hardened, we cannot have His Word penetrate our hearts and become one with Him.

How do you harden your heart? What is blocking God's message from being heard? Is the clatter and noise of the world blocking His voice? Are you more interested in television, the internet, politics, movies, sports, your business or job, or other distractions? Do you give God time in your busy day to talk to you? If not, why not?

Building a relationship with someone is hard if you don't spend time with them. The same is true with your relationship with God. Talk to Him throughout the day. Pray. Meditate on the sufferings of the cross. When times get difficult, insulate yourself in God's love and mercy. Allow Him to wrap His loving arms around you. Be open to God. He loves you more than you can ever imagine. Don't drift from Him. Harden not your heart!

Pray with me: *"In the name of the Father, and of the Son, and of the Holy Spirit. Amen. Christ, our Savior and our King, renew in me allegiance to Your Kingship. I pray for the grace to place You above the powers of this world in all things.*

I pray for the grace to obey You before any civic authority.

I pray for the grace to fervently bring about Your Kingdom in my family and community.

I pray that You will reign in my mind.

I pray that You will reign in my heart.

I pray that You will reign in my will.

I pray that You will reign in my body.

I pray that You will reign throughout all the world.

O Prince of Peace, may Your reign be complete in my life and in the life of the world. Christ, my King.

As I reflect on Your second, glorious coming and the judgment of all mankind, I beg You to show me mercy and give me the grace to become a great saint. I pray that not only will I spend eternity with You but that You may use me – a sinner – to bring others into Your Kingdom for Your glory.

Christ the King, Your Kingdom come!

Amen.

In the name of the Father, and of the Son, and of the Holy Spirit. Amen."

(praymorenoveneas.com)

Chapter 3
Growing Up Catholic

What are your Catholic traditions? If someone came to your house, would they know you are Catholic? If anyone met you on the street, would anything about you indicate you are Catholic? I remember attending a religious education class as a child and was asked, *"If you were put on trial for being Catholic, would they have enough evidence to convict you?"* This question continues to make me reflect on my faith activities. Do people see Christ in me? Do my actions indicate I am a disciple of Jesus Christ? Do yours? Is your heart open to hearing the voice of God and following it? Take a minute to reflect on this.

Growing up Catholic, there were always visible signs in our house showing us we were in a faith-filled home. Every bedroom had a beautiful crucifix over our beds. Our bedroom dresser had a statue of the Infant of Prague facing where we slept. I remember the day the statue fell. It made a loud bang, prompting my mother to run to the bedroom I shared with my sister Lois. My mother asked what happened when she found the statue lying flat on the dresser. My sister exclaimed, *"The ghost must have knocked it over."*

Puzzled, my mother questioned, *"What ghost?"*

My sister said, *"You know, the Holy Ghost!"*

I was glad the Church changed Holy Ghost to Holy Spirit, especially after growing up with the stories of Casper, the friendly ghost!

Infant of Prague: The original statue of the Infant Jesus of Prague was a wedding gift to an Austrian royal family member from her cousin during the 16th century. It was made from wood and covered with wax. The statue's height was almost twenty inches tall. The left hand held a small globe with a cross on top. It was to represent Jesus, the Christ Child, who is king of the entire world. With His right hand, Jesus is blessing those who look at the statue. His first two fingers are raised to represent the two natures of Christ: man and God. The folded thumb and last two fingers touch each other to represent the Father, the Son, and the Holy Spirit in the mystery of the Blessed Trinity.

A Carmelite found the statue years later after it had been damaged and thrown away during the war. He placed the statue in a Carmelite Church in Prague, Czech Republic.

In 1637, Fr. Cyril claimed that the broken statue spoke to him, "*Have mercy on me, and I will have mercy on you. Give me hands, and I will give you peace. The more you honor me, the more I will bless you.*"

The broken hands of the statue were restored. The original statue is preserved in the Carmelite Church of Our Lady of Victory. Many miracles have been recorded and credited to the Infant of Prague. The child Jesus helps us reflect on the Incarnation and reminds us of His humility and willingness to be one of us. When we meditate on this devotion, may we focus on God's great love and ask for humility and smallness.

Pray with me: "*Dearest Jesus, Little Infant of Prague, how tenderly you love us! Your greatest joy is to dwell among us and to bestow your blessing upon us. Though I am not worthy that you should help me, I feel drawn to you by love because you are kind and merciful. So many who turned to you with confidence have received blessings and had their petitions granted. Behold me as I come before you to lay open my heart to you with its prayers and hopes. I present to you, especially this request, which I enclose in Your loving Heart (state your request). Rule over me, dear Infant Jesus, and do with me and mine according to your holy will, for I know that in your divine wisdom and love, you will arrange everything for the best. Do not withdraw your hand from me but protect and bless me forever. I pray you, all-powerful and gracious Infant Jesus, for the sake of your sacred infancy, in the name of your blessed Mother Mary who cared for you with such tenderness and by the greatest reverence with which St. Joseph carried you in his arms, help me in my needs. Make me truly happy with you, dearest Infant, in time and in eternity, and I shall thank you forever with all my heart. Amen."*

One of the bedposts always had plastic rosary beads that would glow in the dark if you hung them over the table lamp before bedtime. A brown scapular also hung on the other bedpost, and we always felt safe going to sleep.

The Rosary: No one knows when the Rosary was first prayed. We know that it became popular thanks to the preaching of Saint Dominic, who died in 1221. He encouraged the Rosary to help teach the foundation of the faith and encourage prayer.

Do you pray the Rosary? It is a powerful way to pray while meditating on the life of Christ. The Joyful Mysteries are meditations on the early years and begin at Jesus' conception when the Angel Gabriel announces to Mary that she will bear a son. The Joyful Mysteries end with Christ as a child, and His parents find Him in the Temple after searching for Him for three days. The Joyful Mysteries are the Annunciation, the Visitation, the Nativity, the Presentation of Our Lord in the Temple, and The Finding of the Child Jesus in the Temple. We pray the Joyful Mysteries on Mondays and Saturdays.

The Luminous Mysteries, also called the Mysteries of Light, were given to us by Pope John Paul II in the early part of this century in the year 2002. It covers Jesus' ministry, starting with the Baptism of Jesus and ending with the Last Supper. The Luminous Mysteries are The Baptism of Jesus in the Jordan, the Wedding Feast at Cana, the Proclamation of the Kingdom of God, the Transfiguration of the Lord, and the Institution of the Holy Eucharist. We pray the Luminous Mysteries on Thursdays.

The Sorrowful Mysteries cover the Passion of Christ and start with the Agony in the Garden, followed by the Scourging at the Pillar, the Crowning with Thorns, the Carrying of the Cross, and the Crucifixion and Death of Our Lord. We pray the Sorrowful Mysteries on Tuesdays and Fridays.

The Glorious Mysteries meditate on the glorious events that happen on Easter and afterward. They are the Resurrection of Christ, the Ascension of Christ into Heaven, the Descent of the Holy Spirit, the Assumption of the Blessed Virgin Mary into Heaven, and the Coronation of the Blessed Virgin as Queen of Heaven and Earth. We pray the Glorious Mysteries on Wednesdays and Sundays.

The Brown Scapular: *Scapular* is a Latin word meaning shoulder blade. It was from the Middle Ages when monks wore them over their clothing. Many people wanted to copy the holy ways of the monks, and the scapular became popular. Made from cloth, the one I wear is no larger than a postage stamp. The ones on my bedposts were larger. The Catholic Church has approved eighteen different scapulars for wear, but the brown scapular is the most popular and is known as the Brown Scapular of Our Lady of Mt. Carmel. It is a devotion to the Blessed Mother.

My mother always placed one on our bedpost with our rosary beads to signify our love for the Blessed Mother. It was **never** considered a good luck charm but rather a devotional. I always felt Mother Mary's love when my head lay on my pillow before I slept.

Let us pray: *"O my God, in union with the Immaculate Heart of Mary (here kiss the Brown Scapular), I offer Thee the Most Precious Body, Blood, Soul and Divinity of Our Lord, Jesus Christ, joining with it my every thought, word, and action of this day. O my Jesus, I desire today to gain every indulgence and merit I can, and offer them, together with myself, to Mary Immaculate, that she may best apply them to the interests of Thy Most Sacred Heart. Amen."*

Going to Mass: My parents always took us to Mass, and every Sunday morning, Dad would line up five quarters on the hallway table so we each had money for the church collection. This weekly routine taught the five of us always to give money to the Church. It was a valuable lesson. Do you teach your children to give to the Church? The cost of living has certainly gone up since I was a child. My daughter gives her children multiple bills to put in the collection box. It is important to teach the gift of giving and teach our children and grandchildren to give generously to the Church.

We had the Catholic Children's Treasure Box books in our house. Each book taught us faith in a fun and straightforward way. My mother also subscribed to a children's monthly magazine called Highlights©. One lesson was called Goofus and Gallant and taught how to make good decisions. Each valuable lesson would help us understand how to do the right thing. My mother took the time to discuss it with us, and I always looked forward to reading these books and magazines. As parents and grandparents, we are called to teach our children and grandchildren how to follow our faith's teachings, spiritually and morally. Do you?

"Let the children come to me; do not prevent them, for the kingdom of God belongs to such as these." (Mark 10: 14) In what ways have you helped bring your children or grandchildren to God? Do you teach them the faith?

TO TEACH IN ORDER TO LEAD OTHERS TO FAITH IS THE TASK OF EVERY PREACHER AND OF EACH BELIEVER.

St. Thomas Aquinas

Do you bring them to Mass? Do you say nightly prayers with your children? Reflect on that now.

Bedtime Prayer for Children

Now I Lay Me Down to Sleep

"Now I lay me down to sleep,
I pray the Lord my soul to keep.
Angels watch me through the night,
And wake me with the morning light."

Chapter 4
Christmas Memories

One of the saddest things to hear about is families who have broken relationships and no longer communicate with each other. Families that were once joyful and loving are now separated and angry. Their hearts are hardened to Jesus' commandment, *"Love one another just as I have loved you!"* (John 13:34) There is no joy, only bitterness and pain. Why?

In most cases, the answer can be found in the sin of pride. People feel their wants and needs are more important than others. Jesus said, *"Unless you turn and become like children, you will not enter the kingdom of Heaven. Whoever humbles himself like this child is the greatest in the kingdom of Heaven."* (Matthew 18:3-4) Children give love freely. They are innocent and loving and don't harbor resentment or anger. Can you remember what it was like to be a child, especially at Christmas? The excitement, joy, awe, and wonder were overwhelming. It was an extraordinary time!

My fondest Christmas memories go back to when I was a child. I am the second oldest of five children, and Dad was the second oldest of ten. Christmas was always a time for family gatherings.

After attending Christmas Mass, we always traveled from the suburbs to visit my grandparents' homes in the city. My parents would plan to go to Dad's parents first and then Mom's parents later in the day. I am one of 48 cousins in Dad's family, so his parents had to coordinate times for visiting since there would not be enough room for forty-eight children and twenty-two adults to gather at the same time! Many of my cousins my age came at the same time as we did. During these Christmas gatherings, we created deep friendships and life-long connections.

Christmas dinner was always with my mother's parents. She was their only daughter, and I was incredibly close to Granny. Afterward, my cousins, who lived downstairs, and those down the street would join us. Mom's two brothers had three kids each, and five were girls! Since no alcohol was ever served at my grandparent's house, and Granny's deep Catholic faith would not permit inappropriate language and misbehavior, our gatherings were always joyful and calm. I do not recall one negative incident despite having eight adults, eleven children, and one dog in a small apartment size house.

I have fond memories of the sounds of laughter, the savory smells of prime rib cooking, and vegetables baking in the oven. I also remember the unforgettable taste of homemade chocolate cake with decadent fudge frosting and warm apple pie made from scratch with melting vanilla ice cream on top. Granny was an incredible baker, and her desserts were always craved and appreciated, but my fondest memories were the hugs of loved ones who are no longer with us today. Christmas was not about the food or the presents under the tree, but the people who gathered to celebrate the joy of family and faith!

What are your fondest Christmas memories? Do you reflect on your family positively and lovingly? We are all called to love one another. *"A new commandment I give to you, that you love one another: just as I have loved you, you also are to love one another."* (John 13:34-35) If you are not celebrating this holy holiday with your family, now might be the time to reconcile and mend family conflicts. Jesus didn't just suggest that we love one another; He commanded it.

I can think of no better time to show our love for each other than Christmas. Christmas is not a time to harden your hearts but to embrace the miracle of God becoming man and dwelling among us.

In 1994, when the Church celebrated the 'Year of the Family," Saint John Paul II wrote at length about the family. He said, *"The civilization of love is possible; it is not a utopia. But it is only possible by a constant and ready reference to the 'Father from whom all fatherhood on Earth is named,' from whom every human family comes."*

Today, let's pray that all families may be more Christ-centered, recognizing all good as gifts from our Father.

Let us pray: "*In the name of the Father, and of the Son, and of the Holy Spirit. Amen.*

Jesus, I trust in You. Please grant through Your mother's intercession that I may always bring Your hope into my family.

Jesus, I trust in You. Please grant through Your mother's intercession that I may always bring Your love into my family.

Jesus, I trust in You. Please grant through Your mother's intercession that I may always bring Your mercy into my family.

Oh, holy Mother, St. Joachim and St. Anne were delighted to love and care for so holy a child. Pray for me that I may show greater charity to my parents and grandparents in word, prayer, and deed.

Dearest Mother, please pray for me and for these my intentions...

(State your intentions)

Hail Mary, full of Grace, the Lord is with thee. Blessed art thou among women, and blessed is the fruit of thy womb, Jesus. Holy Mary, Mother of God, pray for us sinners now and at the hour of our death. Amen.

In the name of the Father, and of the Son, and of the Holy Spirit.

Amen."

(John-Paul & Annie - Praymorenovenas.com)

Chapter 5

Worship & The Mass

My family always attended Mass on Sunday or Saturday evenings. It was a family tradition that never changed, even when we were on vacation. Mom and Dad took the five of us to church and taught us the value of worship and the Mass. Growing up in Massachusetts, we had the Blue Laws, which prohibited stores from opening on Sundays. People were discouraged from working. Sunday was a day of rest, just like the Bible tells us. *"God blessed the seventh day and made it holy because on it he rested from all the work he had done in creation."* (Genesis 2:3)

I have many great memories of visiting with my cousins and feasting on a Sunday dinner with family. Life was simpler back then, but I think we had our priorities in the correct order: faith and family. How do you spend your Sundays?

Do you attend Mass or a prayer and worship service on Sunday or Saturday evenings? Do you take time to pray as a community? Our church is not a building. **We** are the church, and Jesus calls us to pray together!

Every person at the service you attend is your brother or your sister. We form one body, the Body of Christ. Why would anyone not want to be a part of the family of God? At Baptism, you became a child of God. Your name was written in His book.

As a Catholic, I attend Mass every weekend. The Mass and Holy Eucharist give me strength for the week ahead. Whenever I couldn't attend because of sickness or unexpected circumstances, I felt lost during the week. Receiving the Body and Blood of Christ through the Eucharist gave me a shield of protection and strength to deal with the week's challenges. It centered me. I would be lost without Sunday Mass. Do you attend? If not, do you struggle with day-to-day problems? Why would anyone want to go through life without the Lord at their side? Harden not your heart. He loves you and wants to be one with you through the Holy Eucharist.

The miracle that occurs at every Mass is one I never want to miss or take for granted. If we could see what happens during the Mass, we would be overwhelmed to tears and filled with wonder and awe. Catalina Rivas of Cochabamba, Bolivia, witnessed what indeed occurs in the Mass. The Blessed Mother removed the veil from her eyes and allowed her to witness something almost impossible to describe and too long to put into this chapter. She has the approval of her Bishop René Fernandez Apaza, who has given his imprimatur to her messages. I urge you to read her powerful explanation of what really happens during the Mass. Just Google her name.

During the Mass, Heaven and Earth are connected! Your loved ones and all the Saints in Heaven can see you in the pew. How powerful! A choir of angels is present, singing alleluia and blowing their trumpets, praising God. It's a spectacular event.

There are several parts of the Mass. They are the Introductory Rites, Liturgy of the Word, Liturgy of the Eucharist, Communion Rite, and Concluding Rite. The priest is the last person to enter the church. He begins by welcoming everyone to the celebration of the Holy Mass. You are late if you arrive when the priest has already started praying from the altar. Mass usually begins with an entrance hymn. My favorites are *"Gather Us In"* and *"All Are Welcome."*

Before entering the pew, you should genuflect while facing the Tabernacle, then make the Sign of the Cross. Always show reverence to Jesus, who is present in the Holy Tabernacle when the door is closed, and the red sanctuary light is on. The Sign of the Cross is a profession of faith. It is a declaration of our belief in the Father, Son, and Holy Spirit. When I get to my seat, I immediately kneel and pray to God. I am now in His house and presence, so I must greet, praise, and worship Him.

I try to arrive fifteen minutes early to pray and prepare for being in the Real Presence of Jesus. There are several prayers that I recite.

First, I do a sincere Act of Contrition and ask for forgiveness of my sins.

"Oh my God, I am heartily sorry for having offended Thee. I detest all of my sins because I dread the loss of Heaven and the pains of hell, but most of all because I have offended Thee my God, who art all good and deserving of all my love. I firmly resolve with the help of Thy grace to confess my sins, to do penance, and to mend my life, Amen."

Second, I consecrate myself to the Blessed Mother and use this as my offering.

Consecration to the Blessed Mother: "*O, my Queen and my Mother! I offer myself entirely to thee, and, in proof of my filial affection, I consecrate this day (and every day) to thee, my eyes (May I always see my God), my ears (May I always hear the voice of God), my lips (May I always proclaim the Word of God), my heart (May it always be connected to yours), my whole being without reserve. Since I am wholly thine, O bountiful Mother, keep me and defend me as thy property and possession. Amen.*"

Third, I read this prayer by St. Thomas Aquinas.

"Almighty and ever-living God, I approach the sacrament of Thine only begotten Son, our Lord Jesus Christ. I come sick to the doctor of life, unclean to the fountain of mercy, blind to the radiance of eternal light, and poor and needy to the Lord of Heaven and Earth.

"Therefore, I ask in the abundance of Thy great generosity that Thou may heal my sickness, wash away my defilement, enlighten my blindness, enrich my poverty, and clothe my nakedness, so that I may receive the Bread of angels, the King of kings, the Lord of lords, with that reverence and humility, with that contrition and devotion, with that purity and faith, with that purpose and intention which is expedient for the salvation of my soul.

"Grant me, I beseech Thee, that I may not only receive the Sacrament of the Body and Blood of the Lord, but also its reality and power.

"O most kind God, grant that I may receive the Body of Thine only begotten Son, our Lord Jesus Christ, which He received from the Virgin Mary, so that I may be worthy to be incorporated into His Mystical Body, and numbered among His members.

"O most loving Father, grant that I may contemplate for all eternity the revealed face of Thy beloved Son, whom I intend to receive now under the veil of this sacrament.

"Who liveth and reigneth with Thee, world without end. Amen."

I end with the Our Father, Hail Mary, and Glory Be to the Father prayers.

The Mass is like a family gathering. When you gather with family, don't you try to reconcile with any members you may have had a problem with during the week, especially a parent? We do the same when we start the Mass by asking God's forgiveness for anything we have done to offend Him during the week. Venial sins are forgiven during the Penitential Rite.

As with a family gathering, if we committed a significant grievance against a family member, we would meet them face to face and ask for forgiveness to reconcile before gathering with the entire family. So, if our sins are mortal or severe, we need to go to Confession or Reconciliation before attending Mass, especially if we want to receive the Eucharist.

As with family gatherings, we listen to family stories. In Mass we sit and hear two Readings and a Psalm from a Lectionary which is taken from sections of the Bible. A Lectionary comprises the Readings and the Responsorial Psalm assigned for each Mass. The Readings are connected by the theme or celebration of the day. The Sunday Readings are divided into three years and are labeled A, B, and C. Each cycle focuses on a particular Gospel writer.

In Year A, we mostly hear the Gospel of Matthew. In Year B, we hear the Gospel of Mark and chapter 6 of the Gospel of John. In Year C, we hear the Gospel of Luke. The Gospel of John is read during the Easter season in all three years.

The First Reading comes from the Old Testament and connects to the Gospel Reading. It is followed by a Psalm. The Second Reading comes from the New Testament and usually from a letter written to the early church members. Lay members of the church read these, and they are called Lectors.

We then stand for the Gospel Reading from the Gospels of Mark, Luke, Matthew, or John. These are the teachings and words of Jesus Christ and stories of His life and ministry. The Gospels are read by the priest, deacon, or bishop.

If you are attentive to the Readings, you should know your Bible! Fr. Michael Schmitz has the number one podcast in the nation called *"The Bible in a Year."* He is reading and explaining the entire Bible. If you want to understand more about the Bible, I recommend you listen to his podcasts on Youtube.com.

After the Gospel Reading, we sit and the priest, deacon, or bishop gives a Homily, usually based on the Catholic teachings of the meaning of the day's Readings.

We then stand for the Creed. The Nicene Creed is a profession of our faith. All our Catholic beliefs are listed in the Creed. Do you proclaim your faith loudly with the other church community members? I always loved hearing my dad clearly proclaim his faith. Parents and grandparents should proudly and clearly state their faith beliefs when standing for the Creed. Your children and grandchildren are watching, forming memories and future habits. Be a good role model! I've seen people show more pride and conviction at a sports event when saying the pledge of allegiance or singing the Star Spangled Banner than when they proclaim their faith. Why? Have they become lukewarm? Do you remember what was said about lukewarm followers? *"So, because you are lukewarm, neither hot nor cold, I will spit you out of my mouth.* (Revelations 3:16-17)

NICENE CREED

(Professed at Sunday Mass)

"I believe in one God, the Father, Almighty, maker of Heaven and Earth, of all things visible and invisible.

I believe in one Lord Jesus Christ, the Only Begotten Son of God, born of the Father before all ages; God from God; Light from Light, true God from true God, begotten not made, consubstantial with the Father, through Him all things were made. For us men and for our salvation, He came down from Heaven,

(**BOW YOUR HEAD**) *and by the Holy Spirit, was incarnate of the Virgin Mary and became man.*

(Continue without bowing) *For our sake, He was crucified under Pontius Pilate. He suffered, died and was buried, and rose again, on the third day in accordance with the Scriptures. He ascended into heaven and is seated at the right hand of the Father. He will come again in glory to judge the living and the dead, and His kingdom will have no end.*

I believe in the Holy Spirit, the Lord, the Giver of life, who proceeds from the Father and the Son, who with the Father and the Son is adored and glorified, who has spoken through the prophets.

I believe in one, holy, catholic, and apostolic Church. I confess one Baptism for the forgiveness of sins, and I look forward to the resurrection of the dead and the life of the world to come. Amen."

The Incarnation, God becoming man, is an essential belief for Christians. Therefore, a profound bow during the Creed is the way we show its importance.

After the Creed and church petitions is the Offertory. This is when we offer ourselves to God; our sorrows, pain, hopes, sadness, joy, petitions, gifts, financial support, everything! What do you offer at Mass?

Next is the Eucharistic prayer. The priest is acting in the person of Christ when he changes the bread and wine into the Body and Blood of our Lord Jesus Christ. The Church calls this Transubstantiation. It is a mystery, but the reality is we are in the Real Presence of Jesus just as the apostles were at the Last Supper. The Communion host we receive is not a symbol but the Real Body of Christ. We become one with Jesus! The expression, *"You are what you eat,"* never had such a profound meaning.

LET US REJOICE THEN AND GIVE THANKS THAT WE HAVE BECOME NOT ONLY CHRISTIANS, BUT CHRIST HIMSELF. DO YOU UNDERSTAND AND GRASP, BRETHREN, GOD'S GRACE TOWARD US? MARVEL AND REJOICE: WE HAVE BECOME CHRIST. FOR IF HE IS THE HEAD, WE ARE THE MEMBERS; HE AND WE TOGETHER ARE THE WHOLE MAN...THE FULLNESS OF CHRIST THEN IS THE HEAD AND THE MEMBERS. BUT WHAT DOES 'HEAD AND MEMBERS' MEAN? CHRIST AND THE CHURCH.

ST. AUGUSTINE

Next is the Communion Rite, and we all stand for the prayer Jesus gave us, *"The Lord's Prayer."* After, we give a sign of peace to those around us. Then we pray the *"Lamb of God Prayer"* while standing and the *"Communion Prayer"* while kneeling. We are now in the presence of Jesus and should stay on our knees until it's time to go to Communion and receive the Eucharist.

So many people receive the Holy Eucharist as a routine ritual with no joy, wonder, awe, or true understanding of the miracle we are receiving. Christ told St. Faustina how that makes Him feel.

MY DAUGHTER, WRITE THAT IT PAINS ME VERY MUCH WHEN RELIGIOUS SOULS RECEIVE THE SACRAMENT OF LOVE MERELY OUT OF HABIT, AS IF THEY DID NOT DISTINGUISH THIS

> **FOOD. I FIND NEITHER FAITH NOR LOVE IN THEIR HEARTS. I GO TO SUCH SOULS WITH GREAT RELUCTANCE. IT WOULD BE BETTER IF THEY DID NOT RECEIVE ME (DIARY, 1288).**

How do you receive this Blessed Sacrament? Does your heart burn with the fire of love, or have you hardened your heart to Jesus?

> **I DESIRE TO UNITE MYSELF WITH HUMAN SOULS; MY GREAT DELIGHT IS TO UNITE MYSELF WITH SOULS. KNOW, MY DAUGHTER, THAT WHEN I COME TO A HUMAN HEART IN HOLY COMMUNION, MY HANDS ARE FULL OF ALL KINDS OF GRACES WHICH I WANT TO GIVE TO THE SOUL. BUT SOULS DO NOT EVEN PAY ANY ATTENTION TO ME; THEY LEAVE ME TO MYSELF AND BUSY THEMSELVES WITH OTHER THINGS. OH, HOW SAD I AM THAT SOULS DO NOT RECOGNIZE LOVE! THEY TREAT ME AS A DEAD OBJECT (DIARY, 1385).**

We should never leave Mass right after Communion. This is a very holy time. You have just become one with Christ. Take time to pray silently. If the Tabernacle door is open, please stay on your knees. You are in the presence of Christ.

As soon as I receive Communion and return to my pew, I always read this prayer from St. Thomas Aquinas.

"Lord, Father all-powerful and ever-living God, I thank Thee, for even though I am a sinner, Thine unprofitable servant, not because of any merit of my own, but in the kindness of Thy mercy, Thou hast fed me with the precious Body and Blood of Thy Son, our Lord Jesus Christ.

"I pray that this Holy Communion may not bring me condemnation and punishment but forgiveness and salvation.

"May it be an armor of faith and a shield of good will. May it purify me from my vices and put an end to my evil passions.

"May it bring me charity and patience, humility and obedience, and growth in every virtue.

"May it be a firm defense against the wiles of all my enemies, visible and invisible, and the perfect quieting of all my evil impulses, bodily and spiritual. May it unite me more closely to Thee, the one true God, and lead me safely through death to everlasting happiness with Thee.

"And I pray that Thou wilt lead me, a sinner, to that ineffable banquet where Thou, with Thy Son and Holy Spirit, art to Thy Saints true light, total fulfillment, everlasting joy, and perfect happiness.

Grant this through Christ our Lord. Amen."

We should pray each prayer with understanding, faith, and conviction. Are you focused on the words? We are in a community of believers who should praise and adore our Lord and Savior. We should burn with the fire of love. Do you? Are you actively participating? Are you allowing God to move you? To change and transform you? Are you ready to go out and proclaim the Good News of the Gospel? If not, why not? Do you know what the word Mass means? Mass is from the Latin words *"Ite, missa est."* It is more than a dismissal. It's a command to go and proclaim the Word of God. Do you? My favorite recessional hymns are *"Go Make a Difference"* and *"Make Love of God Known."* These hymns or songs are at the end of the Mass and close it.

The priest should always be the first person to leave at the end of the Mass. We should stay in our pew until he processes out. Most priests and pastors will be waiting at the entrance of the church to greet you as you leave. This is not the time to complain to them. You should be filled with joy and love. Smile! Do not harden your heart; instead, be the light of Christ.

> *"Shout joyfully to God, all the Earth, sing of his glorious name, give him glorious praise.*
> *Say to God: "How awesome your deeds!*
> *Before your great strength your enemies cringe.*
> *All the Earth falls in worship before you;*
> *They sing of you, sing of your name!"* (Psalm 66:2-4)

Chapter 6

Seeking God

The desire for God is written in the human heart because man is created by God and for God, and God never ceases to draw man to himself. Only in God will he find the truth and happiness he never stops searching for. (CCC I. 27)

For as long as I can remember, I have always sought God. From my early youth days when I attended weekend retreats to the countless books I read, knowing and seeking God was an essential part of me. I always felt at peace because of my faith in God. The more I studied, prayed, and sought God, the more I thrived in His graces. Do you search for God? Do you spend time in prayer, reflection, and worship? St. Augustine said, *"Lord, you have made us for yourself, and our hearts are restless until they rest in you."*

So many parents have shared with me that their adult children raised in the faith have left the Catholic Church. Their constant prayer is for their children to return to the faith and join them at Mass. Their children have hardened their hearts to God. The noises of the world have blocked out the voice of God. Their restless souls are confused and ache; many have used alcohol, drugs, food, nicotine, and other unhealthy habits to fill this hole.

They are craving something that can never be satisfied without God. We can never get enough of what we don't need. Maybe it is time we fill that void with God.

Bishop Barron understands this and one of his teachings describes the importance of staying focused on God. The devil wants us to be undisciplined and lazy and to stay away from God.

Bishop Robert Barron said it best:

> **"FRIENDS, IN TODAY'S GOSPEL JESUS EXPLAINS THE PARABLE OF THE SOWER. THE SEED SOWN ON THE PATH IS 'THE ONE WHO HEARS THE WORD WITHOUT UNDERSTANDING IT, AND THE EVIL ONE COMES AND STEALS AWAY WHAT WAS SOWN.' THIS MEANS WE MIGHT END UP BLOCKED FROM GOD BECAUSE WE LACK EDUCATION IN THE WAYS OF THE SPIRIT.**
>
> **THE SEED SOWN ON ROCKY GROUND IS 'THE ONE WHO HEARS THE WORD AND RECEIVES IT AT ONCE WITH JOY. BUT HE HAS NO ROOT AND LASTS ONLY FOR A TIME.' WHEN DIFFICULTIES AND PERSECUTIONS ARRIVE, HE LOSES CONFIDENCE.**
>
> **THE SEED SOWN AMONG THORNS IS THE ONE WHO HEARS THE WORD, BUT THEN WORLDLY ANXIETY AND THE LURE OF RICHES CHOKE THE WORD, AND IT BEARS NO FRUIT.' SOME PEOPLE HEAR THE WORD, BUT THEN THEY ARE UNABLE TO MAINTAIN THEIR FOCUS AND SENSE OF PRIORITIZATION.**

SO FROM THESE SAD CASES, WE CAN CONSTRUE THE NATURE OF GOOD SOIL. WHEN WE UNDERSTAND THE FAITH, WHEN WE TAKE THE TIME TO READ THEOLOGY, TO STUDY THE SCRIPTURES; WHEN WE PERSEVERE, DISCIPLINE OURSELVES, AND PRACTICE THE FAITH; WHEN WE HAVE OUR PRIORITIES STRAIGHT; THEN THE SEED WILL TAKE ROOT IN US. AND IT WILL BEAR FRUIT THIRTY, SIXTY, OR A HUNDREDFOLD."

BISHOP BARRON

***

We need to spend time in prayer. Do you pray? St. Monica prayed for her husband and son to become believers. She prayed for seventeen years for her son St. Augustine's conversion and endlessly for her husband and mother-in-law before they converted. She never gave up! Most mothers love their children unconditionally. The Blessed Mother loves her children, too. If you pray the Rosary, why not add the following prayer:

"With this Rosary, I bind my children and grandchildren to the Immaculate Heart of Mary for her guidance and protection."

Let us pray for the return of non-practicing Catholics:

"O Good Shepherd, you never cease to seek out the lost, to call home the stray, to comfort the frightened, and to bind up the

wounded. I ask you to bring (names) back to the practice of the Faith and to remove all obstacles that prevent them from receiving your abundant mercy, which flows sacramentally through the heart of your holy Church. Through the intercession of Mary, the Mother of God, their Guardian Angels, their Patron Saints, and the ever-prayerful St. Monica, may you pardon their sins and unshackle them from whatever hinders their freedom to come Home. For you, O Good Shepherd, have loved us to the end and offered yourself to the father for the salvation of all. Amen."

(https://www.dioceseofflansing.org)

Chapter 7

Traveling with Praise & Worship

When you travel, do you look for ways to show God's love? Are you open to being an apostle of Christ? Do you take advantage of the opportunity to spread the Word of God, or do you harden your heart and avoid sharing your faith? We are all called to be God's hands, feet, and voice. Next time you travel, think about making it an exceptional Christian vacation experience!

I am always looking for vacations with praise and worship. It all began with my husband, John. He tried to convince me to move to Florida in 1988 and used the rationale of meeting people and making friends while he was young to have these friends when he retired. He did not want to retire to Florida and not know anyone. I use that same rationale when choosing our vacation plans. Our final destination is Heaven, and I want to meet people who share the same goal. Imagine being surrounded by all those you love and care about in Paradise! How can you not have joy when you bring God into your travel plans?

John and I booked a Caribbean Cruise with Christian singer and songwriter Michael W. Smith and friends for July 19-26, 2008. This seven-day cruise aboard the Carnival Liberty left Miami,

Florida, and traveled to Cozumel, Mexico, the Grand Cayman Islands, and Ocho Rios, Jamaica. Michael traveled with his family and friends, including singer and songwriter Amy Grant, comedian Jeff Allen, and the American Idol finalist Melinda Doolittle. I was more excited about the journey than the destination. Someone asked me where the cruise was traveling to, and my response was, *"I don't care where it's going. We can go in circles for all I care. I'm going to be listening to Michael W. Smith!"*

It was apparent that I was filled with joy and excitement. I am always amazed at how God orchestrates our lives and the many blessings He showers on us. John and I met many beautiful people on the cruise, including a special couple from California, Rick and Sally Cryder. Sally had an inner glow of joy, and her smile was contagious. She always lit up the room when she entered, making us feel like family. We became instant friends. We learned that Rick and Sally had a non-profit group called Angels of Love (www.angelsoflove.org). Rick and Sally established Angels of Love in 1997 as a ministry to comfort people suffering from a serious illness like cancer, a disability, tragedy, or the death of a family member. They and their wonderful volunteers donated their time and talent to make beautiful stained glass, gold-plated Angels of Love to give encouragement, love, and comfort. Once Rick heard my dad had died from cancer, he presented me with one of these beautiful Angels of Love. This is a cherished gift that I look at almost every day. They asked us to join them when they presented an Angel of Love to Michael W. Smith! After hearing about another person on the cruise diagnosed with cancer, they invited us to go to this person's cabin to pray over him and present him with an Angel of Love. We were blessed to be a part of this ministry, if only for a short time on the cruise ship.

Do you allow God to guide you wherever you are, at home or on vacation? Are you open to sharing God's love? When was the last time someone asked you to join them in prayer? Were you open to it? Have you ever laid your hands on someone and prayed for them? If not, why not? St. Paul tells us to pray without ceasing. *"Pray without ceasing. In all circumstances give thanks, for this is the will of God for you in Christ Jesus."* (1 Thessalonians 5: 17-18)

In one of our many conversations, I shared with Sally that my Christmas morning ritual was listening to Michael W. Smith's song "*Gloria*" at full volume. The song always filled me with joy and praise. The electrifying sounds of praise and worship that gave glory to God on this special and holy day were so powerful when it was played loudly. It also woke my sleeping teenagers up to open Christmas presents. Sally was not familiar with the song or the Christmas CD. When we gave Michael the Angel of Love, I asked him to play "*Gloria*" at the evening concert. He smiled and reminded me that he had a full orchestra and choir for backup for the CD. *"Of course! That's what makes the song so powerful and moving!"* I laughed and agreed with him that it wouldn't be possible and then said I would buy them the CD to hear it at home.

Are you open to sharing things that bring you joy and a closeness to God? Do you share your faith with others? Do you provide tools to others to help them in their faith journey?

That night Michael played just enough chords of *"Gloria"* so I could recognize it. I was bursting with joy over the kind gesture. Michael had the opportunity to brighten my evening, and he did. He has a strong love for God in his heart. The entire cruise was so joyful as we gave God praise and worship.

Oh, and that comment about going in circles, I had to laugh out loud when I saw that our ship was going in circles over Cuba to avoid Hurricane Dolly going through the Gulf of Mexico when it left Cancun and headed for Texas as a Category 2 Hurricane. Michael and his musicians were gallant in playing their music on a very rocky and turbulent stage as the ship swayed back and forth in the choppy waters. I do not think any of us were afraid. We knew God was with us!

As a footnote to my sweet memory, while writing this book, I was informed of the passing of Sally. She fought a courageous battle with cancer and died on Sunday, December 5, 2021, leaving family and friends who loved her. Sally was a compassionate and caring person who lived her faith daily. I know she is in the loving arms of Jesus and enjoying the fruits of Heaven.

Let us pray: "*We give them back to thee, dear Lord, who gavest them to us: Yet as thou dost not lose them by their return. Not as the world giveth, givest thou, O Lover of Souls. What thou gavest, thou takest not away. For what is thine is ours also if we are thine. And Life is eternal, and Love is immortal, and death is only an horizon, and an horizon is nothing save the limit of our sight. Lift us up, strong Son of God, that we may see further; cleanse our eyes that we may see more clearly; draw us closer to thyself so that we may know ourselves to be nearer to our loved ones who are with thee. And while thou dost prepare a place, that where thou art we may also be evermore.*"

William Penn (1644-1718)

Chapter 8
Seeking the Company of the Faithful

St. Augustine said, *"Lord, you have made us for yourself, and our hearts are restless until they rest in you."* Do you have a deep longing to know God? Do you feel a magnetic draw when you want to know more about God? One that is so powerful it makes you move out of your comfort zone. I have!

I presented the Word on Fire *"Catholicism"* series at Epiphany Cathedral to the staff and parishioners in 2011. I was overwhelmed by the powerful teachings of then Fr. Robert Barron. His intense love for the faith and his eloquent language when describing it required me always to have a dictionary nearby. Fr. Barron is gifted with an exceptional vocabulary and a profound way with words. I loved reading his books and listening to his CDs, but his videos utterly moved me. He brought our Catholic faith to life. I had a strong desire to meet him.

I decided to contact the regional manager for Lighthouse Catholic Media, Julie Musselman, where I was purchasing Fr. Barron's CDs. We had never met, but I had her contact information from my purchase orders. The sweet voice on the other end did not hesitate to assist me when I called.

I asked, *"How can I meet Fr. Barron? I want to invite him to speak at my school."*

I had successfully booked Mathew Kelly from Dynamic Catholic, Curtis Martin from FOCUS, Fr. Don Calloway, and Fr. Michael Gaitley to come and speak. Their talks blessed our parish and families, and I had hoped to do the same with Fr. Barron. Little did I know how unrealistic this wish was since he was becoming known internationally and was in great demand.

Julie mentioned that Lighthouse Catholic Media was having its annual leadership conference on October 13 -16, 2011, at the University of St. Mary of the Lake, Mundelein Seminary near Chicago, and Fr. Barron was one of the keynote speakers. She invited me to join her as her guest, to my amazement and joy. Of course, I said yes. I think I shocked myself since I rarely traveled without my husband – especially since 9/11 – and all the airport security that was now in place because of it. But I excitedly agreed to meet her for the first time at the airport.

I stayed overnight at a hotel near the Tampa airport to avoid the morning commuter traffic and to be on time for the early flight. Julie had others joining her, and I quickly became part of a beautiful spirit-filled group heading to a fantastic experience.

God blessed me with so many beautiful memories and friendships that long weekend. My biggest surprise came when Julie offered me her seat at the table for a private luncheon with Fr. Barron. Several people had earned this coveted honor through their efforts in the organization, and this beautiful soul gave me her well-deserved award. I was humbled and honored and will always be grateful for her generous heart. God does put beautiful people in our lives if we are open to them. How many times do we harden our hearts to these gifts? How often do we take them for granted or think we are lucky? God gives us graces every day! Take time to open your heart and give Him thanks and praise.

During the luncheon, I tried to convince Fr. Barron to come to Epiphany and speak. My usual negotiation skills fell flat, and I was humbled learning that his audiences now are in the thousands and his mission to evangelize was sending him to countries worldwide. I truly felt like I was in the presence of a future saint. His Word on Fire ministry was indeed on fire with the Holy Spirit. It was not long before he left Mundelein Seminary after serving as their rector and became the auxiliary bishop of the Archdiocese of Los Angeles.

If you are unfamiliar with the *"Catholicism"* series, I highly recommend you watch it. His Word on Fire website has many more programs: www.wordonfire.org

You can also find many great podcasts by Bishop Barron on www.youtube.com.

In 2015 Lighthouse Catholic Media merged with the Augustine Institute. They offer fantastic teaching tools, including the program FORMED.org.

These wonderful sites and programs were created to help you and me grow in our faith. Take time to check them out. Their videos will fill your mind and thoughts with the Word of God and are far better than anything that you may watch on TV or at secular movies.

St. Augustine says: *"Thou hast made us for thyself, O Lord, and our heart is restless until it finds its rest in thee."* God created that longing in each of us. Do not let the world block it out. Harden not your hearts, but instead seek God!

Pray with me the **St. Augustine's Prayer to the Holy Spirit**:

Breathe in me, O Holy Spirit, that my thoughts may all be holy; Act in me, O Holy Spirit, that my works, too, may be holy; Draw my heart O Holy Spirit, that I love but what is holy; Strengthen me, O Holy Spirit, to defend all that is holy; Guard me then, O Holy Spirit, that I always may be holy.

With Bishop Robert Barron

Chapter 9

St. André

One of my fondest memories growing up with Mom and Granny was hearing all the stories about St. Joseph's Oratory in Montreal, Canada, where Granny was raised. Mom would share the stories of how Granny would climb the stairs leading to the St. Joseph Oratory on her knees. I was always fascinated by her deep faith and that of her mother. I knew just enough to be curious but not enough to be satisfied. I wanted to learn more about St. André, whose heart is displayed in this remarkable shrine on top of a hill.

Traveling to Montreal was always on my bucket list, and John and I decided to book a tour in 2014. The bus tour left Boston and was to head to Montreal, Canada, with several other stops on the itinerary, including Niagara Falls. I was excited about this adventure. Unfortunately, I picked the wrong tour company. The driver's determination to cut costs once the bus left Boston caused him to change many of the scheduled plans. Instead of the first-night stay at Niagara Falls, he went directly to Montreal, Canada, and proceeded to rush through the places we were expecting to see. The driver informed us that our visit to St. Joseph's Oratory would be a brief 30 minutes. I did not keep my disappointment to myself, and once others knew that I wanted to spend more time there, they joined my husband and me in requesting a more extended stay. Two women on the bus who were instrumental in convincing the driver to spend two hours instead of thirty minutes were not Catholic but enjoyed learning about St. André and the Catholic faith. I will be forever grateful for their help.

St. André was born in Quebec, Canada, on August 9, 1845. His parents named him Alfred Bessette, and he was a very sickly baby. The doctors warned his parents that he probably would not survive more than a few days. Thankfully, God had other plans! Although he was sickly most of his life, St. André lived to the ripe old age of 91.

He grew up with little formal education. His childhood pastor encouraged him to seek religious life. He sent him to the congregation of the Holy Cross with a note that said, *"I am sending you a saint."* At first, they did not accept him due to his poor health and lack of education. On December 27, 1870, he was accepted, thanks to the endorsement of the Archbishop of Montreal. He took the name André in honor of his childhood pastor. Because of his limitations, he was assigned to be the doorkeeper of Notre Dame College in Montreal. This position allowed him to greet visitors and interact with all who came for aid. As a brother, he prayed for the intercession of St. Joseph when people asked for prayers. Many people were healed, and word spread quickly of his healing powers. Brother André remained humble and always gave credit and praise to St. Joseph. This inspired him to save his earnings and build a small shrine in St. Joseph's honor. It was finished in 1904, and Brother Andre' was assigned as the caretaker of the Oratory of St. Joseph.

Because of the large number of people who visited to seek the *"Miracle Man of Montreal,"* a larger basilica was constructed. It's estimated that thousands of healings occurred due to his prayers. Brother André died on January 6, 1937. It was estimated that one million people attended despite the harsh winter weather of Canada. On October 17, 2010, St. André Bessette became the first Congregation of Holy Cross saint when Pope Benedict XVI canonized him.

I am grateful to my granny, who shared with me her faith, especially the story of St. André.

In honor of my mother and my granny, let us pray:

"Today, let us pray for all mothers and grandmothers, in thanksgiving for their sacrifices that have benefited us all, and that they may be rewarded with God's mercy and grace.

"In the name of the Father, and of the Son, and of the Holy Spirit. Amen.

"O St. Anne, you are my spiritual grandmother.

"Please pray for me!

"I come to you today asking that you pray for me to see God's goodness in my life, just the way that it is.

"It is easy for me to forget about the blessings that do exist in my life while I pray for another one.

"It is easy for me to forget about the beauty that does exist in my life while I focus on what is lacking.

"Instead, I ask you to please pray for me today that I may be present in each moment and that I may be open to seeing God's goodness, beauty, and loving hand in my day – just as it is.

"Please pray that I may be able to live in the present, and not to dwell on the past or the future.

"Please pray for...

(Mention your intentions here).

"But most of all, please pray that I may be open to God's will the way that you were and that I will be able to wait with patience, perseverance in faith and hope, and with absolute trust in the Lord's plan for me. Amen.

"In the name of the father, and of the Son, and of the Holy Spirit. Amen."

(John-Paul & Annie - Praymorenovenas.com)

Chapter 10
Finding God in Our Travels

Are you open to God's voice? Do you allow Him to talk to you? What do you do to seek Him? Is He always on your mind and in your heart? If not, why not? God loves you so much! He wants to walk and talk to you. Do not harden your heart. Take a minute to invite God into your day, into your thoughts, and into your heart.

John and I loved to travel before Covid-19 hit and restricted our traveling. Before 2020 we would take one or two cruises a year. Do you love to travel? What activities do you search for when you travel? I am always drawn to the churches, especially the Catholic churches! When we find one, John and I take time to go in and pray. This spiritual time always fills us with joy and peace.

When we traveled to San Juan, Puerto Rico, I asked John if we could look for the Cathedral Basilica Minor de San Juan Bautista, built-in 1521. It was on the tour guide's list of must-see places. This cathedral has almost 500 years of history, and after being destroyed in a storm, it was rebuilt in 1529. It is considered the second-oldest cathedral in the Americas and has the tomb of founder Ponce de Leon. I did not want to pay for a time constraint tour but instead be able to walk through at my own pace. Although I had a map, I was confused about the directions, and we became lost. We stood on the street trying to figure out which way to go when a stranger approached us. His clothes and appearance might indicate that he was either homeless or needed financial help. He smiled and offered his assistance. My first inclination was that he was probably looking for a handout in exchange for directions. I was about to discover that I was completely wrong in my assumption.

When I mentioned we were looking for the cathedral, he noticed the miraculous medal around my neck.

"Are you Catholic?" he inquired.

"Why yes, we are!" I responded.

He gave us directions to the cathedral but mentioned another church we needed to see first. He said it was nearby and to follow him. I wrestled with myself on whether it was safe to follow him, but something reassured me not to worry. I could have hardened my heart from fear by not accepting this man's invitation to follow him, but I did not. I felt the presence of God and was open to the graces He wanted to send me. I am glad we went.

He led us to a church not far from where we were standing. It was the *Parroquia* San Francisco de Asis Catholic Church. I would not have known it was a church from the outside. When we went inside, stairs led us down into an underground cemetery or catacomb with vaults. He took the time to explain the story of all the vaults. They contained the remains of those who died many years ago. Like an experienced tour guide, he gave us a beautiful history of the people of Puerto Rico. When he was finished, he directed us upstairs to the main church and altar. Beautiful statues lined the walls, including one of St. Francis. I would never have found this special place on my own. Before I could thank the man, who led us there, he had gone into a pew on the left to pray. John and I went into the pew on the right side and closer to the altar to pray. After we said our prayers and were done, I turned to give the kind man a tip for helping us, but I could not find him. He was gone. I have often thought of him and wondered if God had sent us an angel to direct our path. We eventually found the cathedral, but the first church was the true treasure!

Pray with me: "*Dear Lord Jesus, I have specific requests that may only partially fill the infinite needs and desires that are in my heart. I ask that You answer me not only for those requests but also for a greater reliance on You to satisfy the needs and desires that You have given me. May I seek You with a sincere heart, knowing that it will profit me nothing if I gain the whole world yet lose my soul. Help me to see Your blessings in every day, and help me to love You more. Thank You for everything, Lord Jesus! Amen.*"

(John-Paul & Annie - Praymorenovenas.com)

Chapter 11
Surrendering to God

What do you do when you are given unexpected news that brings you anxiety and fear? Maybe you were given news of a job loss, a health scare, or a friend or family member needing prayers. Do you panic? Do you get an upset stomach or headache? These are all common reactions to stress, but Jesus commands us, "*Be not afraid.*" (Luke 12:20) He said to His disciples, "*Therefore I tell you, do not be anxious about your life.*" And again, He said, "*Fear not.*" (Matthew 10:31)

When I first heard these words, I was pretty conflicted. It is our human nature to have these reactions to fear. One of my faith books told me to give God all my problems and concerns. My first thought was, *"No, I can't do that!"* My strong Irish will did not want to let go of my control over my emotions and fears. I remember saying no. God was patient with me. He knew I had to mature more in my faith. It wasn't until years later that I finally understood what it meant to surrender everything to God completely. "*Not my will Lord, but Your will be done!*" Once I realized I was limited in what I could do, but God could do everything, I learned to pray and give all I had to Him. Once I did, I finally understood the Beatitude, *"Blessed are the meek, for they shall inherit the Kingdom of God."* I always thought meek meant quiet and non-combative. It doesn't. In ancient Greece, war horses were trained to be meek, which meant strong and powerful yet under control and willing to submit. It's steady courage. A meek person doesn't shy from standing up for their beliefs. They do it in a controlled and appropriate way. God wants us to submit and be transformed to His holy will.

> **ONE OF THE MOST FUNDAMENTAL STATEMENTS OF FAITH IS THIS: YOUR LIFE IS NOT ABOUT YOU. YOU'RE NOT IN CONTROL. THIS IS NOT YOUR PROJECT. RATHER, YOU ARE PART OF GOD'S GREAT DESIGN. TO BELIEVE THIS IN YOUR BONES AND ACT ACCORDINGLY IS TO HAVE FAITH. WHEN WE OPERATE OUT OF THIS TRANSFORMED VISION, AMAZING THINGS CAN HAPPEN, FOR WE HAVE SURRENDERED TO "A POWER ALREADY AT WORK IN US THAT CAN DO INFINITELY MORE THAN WE CAN ASK OR IMAGINE." EVEN A TINY BIT OF FAITH MAKES AN EXTRAORDINARY DIFFERENCE.**
>
> **BISHOP BARRON**

***

When we give God control of our lives, we invite Him into our hearts and open our ears to hear His voice! This act of surrendering everything to God is life-changing.

Pray with me the surrender prayer:

"O Jesus, I surrender myself to You; take care of everything!"

Chapter 12
Hurricane Dorian

What are you afraid of? Is there something that makes you fearful? Bishop Barron teaches us to address our fears as a spiritual question.

> "WHO OR WHAT ARE YOU AFRAID OF? THAT IS A VERY IMPORTANT SPIRITUAL QUESTION. ONE WAY TO UNDERSTAND OUR LIVES IS TO LOOK AT THOSE THINGS THAT WE SEEK: WEALTH, POWER, PRIVILEGE, HONOR, PLEASURE, FRIENDSHIP. BUT ANOTHER WAY IS TO TURN THAT QUESTION AROUND AND DETERMINE WHAT OR WHO IT IS THAT WE FEAR.
>
> WE MIGHT FEAR THE LOSS OF MATERIAL THINGS, THE LOSS OF A JOB, THE LOSS OF PHYSICAL HEALTH, THE LOSS OF THE ESTEEM OF OTHERS, THE LOSS OF PERSONAL INTIMACY, OR ULTIMATELY, THE LOSS OF LIFE ITSELF. WE ARE AFRAID OF MANY THINGS, BUT I'D BE WILLING TO BET THAT THERE IS A PRIMARY OR PRINCIPAL FEAR. WHAT IS IT FOR YOU?
>
> NOW, AFTER IDENTIFYING THAT, LISTEN TO JESUS: "PEACE I LEAVE WITH YOU; MY PEACE I GIVE TO YOU. NOT AS THE WORLD GIVES DO I GIVE IT TO YOU. DO NOT LET YOUR HEARTS BE TROUBLED OR AFRAID." ANY AND ALL OF THE THINGS THAT WE CUSTOMARILY FEAR—LOSS OF MONEY, FAME, PLEASURE, AND POWER—HAVE TO DO WITH THIS WORLD. WHAT JESUS IS

SAYING IS THAT WE SHOULD NOT LET THOSE FEARS COME TO DOMINATE OR DEFINE OUR LIVES, FOR HE IS WITH US—AND WITH HIM IS HIS PEACE." BISHOP ROBERT BARRON

Every year on Labor Day weekend, our oldest daughter and her family take my husband and me on a three-night vacation to the Disney World resorts. It is a birthday celebration for me even though my birthday falls on the last day of September. My birthday celebrations have taken us to the villas in Animal Kingdom, where we have been face-to-face with the giraffes from our second-story balcony. We've also been to the Villas at Wilderness Lodge and the cabins at Fort Wilderness. The weekends are filled with fun and excitement as we dine with the Disney characters and get their pictures and autographs. The grandkids aren't the only ones having a great time!

In 2019 Jill decided instead of the usual Disney World adventure, we would go on a Disney Cruise, and she booked us all on the Disney Dream. She kept this information from me until she announced it on Mother's Day. My only concern was Labor Day weekend fell during hurricane season in Florida.

Weeks before the weekend approached, no storms were on the horizon due to the dry air coming off Africa. I was optimistic that our weekend would be safe. I was wrong.

During the week leading up to Labor Day weekend, Hurricane Dorian formed in the Atlantic. This quickly formed hurricane became a category five, the highest category of hurricanes. Hurricane Dorian was the first major hurricane of the 2019 Atlantic hurricane season, with maximum sustained winds of 185 mph. Its target was the Bahamas, the area for our cruise destination. I have been on two cruises affected by distant hurricanes, and the rough seas made many on the ship seasick. This was different. Hurricane Dorian was a powerful storm, and we would be in its direct line. To my surprise, Disney did not cancel the cruise, so I told my daughter I did not see how we could consider going on it. Without hesitation, my daughter announced that she and her family would be going. Her strong trust in Disney and her confidence that they would protect her and her family gave me a moment of pause. Why don't we have that kind of trust in God? Why don't we have the courage that He will protect us? I turned to my husband and said, "*We are going on the cruise. I will put my trust in God.*" I also wanted to be with my family instead of worrying about them at home.

How many times do we have complete trust in God? Do you surrender everything to Him, or do you harden your hearts and live in fear? Our faith in God should not be reserved for just Sundays but lived every day. As I thought about the potential waves in the ocean we would be traveling on, I was reminded of when the

Apostles were frightened in their rocking boat, and Jesus woke up and calmed the waters. *"He woke up, rebuked the wind, and said to the sea, "Quiet! Be still!" The wind ceased, and there was great calm. Then he asked them, "Why are you terrified? Do you not yet have faith?" They were filled with great awe and said to one another, "Who then is this whom even wind and sea obey?"* (Mark 4: 39-41) Where are you in your trust in the Lord? Do you live in fear? Maybe it is time to turn all your fears over to God and completely trust in His love and mercy.

Disney was on top of things, just as my daughter had anticipated. They made the wise decision to turn our eastern Caribbean cruise into a western Caribbean trip. Although the first night was a little rocky as the Disney Dream sailed along the eastern part of Florida, it quickly headed into the Gulf of Mexico and out of harm's way. The weather in Mexico was beautiful, and we enjoyed each day. We didn't expect the news that the hurricane had stalled off the coast of Florida and that it was too dangerous to return on Labor Day. Our short three-day cruise would become a fabulous full-week cruise courtesy of Disney. They continued to treat us to outstanding entertainment, great food, and a memorable vacation at no extra charge! I am so glad I didn't harden my heart to fear because I would have missed out on this fantastic gift from my daughter.

Jesus loves us more than we can ever imagine. Trust in God in all things. Do not live with fear. Jesus, I trust in you! Pray with me: "*Thank you, Lord, for protecting me and keeping me safe from danger! Forgive me when I become fearful and lose trust in You. Help me never to harden my heart to Your love and mercy. May I always listen to Your voice! Amen*"

Chapter 13

Bedtime Rosary & Prayers

Have you ever been asked to join a prayer group, recite a Rosary, or pray the Divine Mercy Chaplet with others? Did you say yes, or were you too busy? Too tired? Did watching TV, a movie, or playing computer games seem more enticing? Harden not your heart!

> **HOW CAN I LEARN TO PRAY? BY PRAYING IN FELLOWSHIP. PRAYER IS ALWAYS BY PRAYING WITH SOMEONE... I LEARN TO PRAY BY PRAYING WITH OTHERS, WITH MY MOTHER, FOR INSTANCE, FOLLOWING HER WORDS, WHICH ARE GRADUALLY FILLED OUT WITH MEANING FOR ME AS I SPEAK, LIVE, AND SUFFER IN FELLOWSHIP WITH HER. JOSEPH RATZINGER (BENEDICT XVI) FROM HIS BOOK *THE FEAST OF FAITH***

The devil wants you to become lukewarm and lazy. He will put plenty of things in your path to steer you away from praise and worship. Do not let him win! There is nothing more rewarding than praying, and there is nothing more powerful than praying with others, especially dedicated prayer warriors. I will share the story of the amazing graces I received by joining a powerful group of prayer warriors. As a bonus, I will also share with you the words of our Blessed Mother that were given to one of our prayer warriors in daily interior locutions.

An interior ***locution*** *is a mystical concept used by various religions, including the Roman* ***Catholic*** *Church.*
In an interior ***locution****, a person reportedly receives a set of (usually auditory) ideas, thoughts, or imaginations from an outside spiritual source. Interior* ***locutions*** *are most often reported during prayers.*
https://www.voicesireland.com/interior-locution/

I met Barbara Serba a few months before the 2020 COVID -19 virus pandemic hit and before we were all in lockdown. She had moved to Sarasota from Texas, and we shared many mutual interests. Her husband transferred his membership to my husband's Knights of Columbus, and Barb became a member of my Ladies Auxiliary at St. Patrick's Church. We invited her to attend a Divine Mercy Cenacle meeting. At the meeting, she told us about a group of prayer warriors planning to meet each night on Zoom to pray the Rosary and Divine Mercy Chaplet. She said the group would be called Bedtime Rosary and Prayers, and we were invited to join. Because people from across the nation would be participating, there were people online from all four time zones. Because of this, we had to start at 10 PM since we were on Eastern Daylight Time. Our west coast members were praying at 7 PM.

Most of our Divine Mercy Cenacle group felt it was too late for them to start praying, knowing it would go past 11:00 PM, although several did join. Since I am a night person and rarely go to bed before midnight since I retired, this was not an issue for me. The Bedtime Rosary and Prayer group started on April 18, 2020.

Schools and churches closed almost overnight that year, and the need for computer cameras and microphones exceeded the available supplies. Cameras that initially sold for $30-$40 were now going for over $100 on eBay. I had a microphone but no camera those first few months. I could see the members, but they could not see me until June, when I finally was the winning bidder on eBay and paid top dollar for a camera.

I met the core people who formed this prayer group. Most of these women are members of Magnificat. Magnificat is a ministry to Catholic women whose purpose is to help Catholic women have a deeper relationship with God through Jesus and the Holy Spirit. Carolyn Wright from Birmingham, Alabama, is the founder and coordinator of Bedtime Rosary and Prayers. She had talked to Barb and other close friends about starting the group. Praying the Rosary and Divine Mercy Chaplet is always easier when praying with others. I do not think she realized that it would also become our lifeline to connect us with others during this lockdown. For many, the faces they saw on Zoom were the only faces they saw that day. This core group of faithful prayer warriors showed up nightly, and during the first year, they did not miss one day, including Thanksgiving, Christmas, New Year, and Easter!

In the beginning, we brought our nightly prayer petitions, prayed, and talked afterward. Most nights, I was on until after midnight. The group kept getting larger as more people were invited. Many people came when they could, but we always had a solid core group in attendance.

Our leader, Carolyn, was diagnosed with breast cancer. Despite her surgery, chemotherapy, injections, and radiation therapy the first year, she never missed a meeting. On one or two rare occasions, she did have to turn the meeting over to someone and leave early, but she was relentless in making sure we always met. She is the strong and fearless leader of our group!

It did not take long before we became like family. The lockdown from COVID-19 kept us inside our homes, so we all cherished the special time we had to see and visit each other. The prayer warriors came from Vermont, Illinois, Kentucky, South Carolina, Alabama, Florida, Texas, Washington, Montana, Arizona, Nebraska, and Iowa. Several priests joined us when they could.

As Carolyn's treatments increased, she felt we needed to meet earlier. Our prayer time was moved to 9:00 PM, and our petitions started earlier, which helped keep us on task and ended earlier. The time change allowed more of our friends to join in.

The best part of the night, for me, was hearing all the amazing prayers of thanksgiving for answered prayers. God was blessing us with many miracles. When this book went to the publisher, we passed Day 950!

One of our members revealed that she was receiving interior locutions from the Blessed Mother regarding our prayer group. She shared them with us. This member has permitted me to share them with you but has asked to be kept anonymous. I have included three in this chapter and placed additional ones in the appendix at the back of the book. You can believe that the Blessed Mother is speaking, or you can choose not to believe, but her words are beautiful and meaningful. Harden not your hearts. Mother Mary gave us a special gift!

We begin each evening with the Unity Prayer. This beautiful prayer was scribed by Elizabeth Kindelmann (1913-1985), a mystic and founder of the Flame of Love Movement. It is to bind Satan so that souls will not be led into sin. (From *The Flame of Love* by Elizabeth Kindelmann).

Let us pray the Unity Prayer:

"In the name of the Father, Son, and Holy Spirit,
May our feet journey together
May our hands gather in unity
May our hearts beat in unison
May our souls be in harmony
May our thoughts be as one

May our ears listen to the silence together
May our glances profoundly penetrate each other
May our lips pray together to gain mercy
from the Eternal Father."

Interior Locutions During Praying of the Rosary

"Each time you pray the Rosary, another coronation occurs. Instead of twelve stars, each Hail Mary is another rose for my crown; thank you for praying so devoutly and sincerely tonight. I am your Heavenly Mother, and I love each of you; you have formed a cenacle of prayer that meets more frequently than any other prayer group. Your prayers and your requests are each being taken to my Son every evening. He answers each of them. As things become more difficult in your world, remember to always to gather and to pray together like this evening, I must leave you now but know I am always with you. I am Mary."

Scribed on 2/7/2021.

"My beloved daughters of our most perfect Father, God of all goodness and perfection, be at peace. Each of you is being sent certain sufferings, each conducive to bringing you the greatest treasure of all – a more perfectly formed character. My Son, through His chosen ones and the power of the Holy Spirit, instructed His chosen convert, St. Paul, that suffering produces endurance and endurance produces character. Do not attempt to

weigh and measure who among you is shouldering the greatest burden – it is a mere thimbleful compared to the suffering my Son bore for each of you. He would undergo such suffering, again, willingly, just for you – so great is His love for you alone! He desires that you spend an eternity with Him. If it takes suffering to perfect you – so be it. Embrace it with great love and without complaint.

"Remember each other throughout the day with great love and compassion for each other. Know with certainty that our beloved Father will never imperil your spirit. He is with you at every moment of the day. Share your trials and tribulations with Him. He desires to have you converse every intimate detail of your life with Him – both the triumphs and the trials.

"The Trinity is pleased to hear and answer each request as the Father deems is best for each person's ultimate well-being. Do not second guess Our Lord. He is perfect Love.

"Thank you for your presence at the cenacle tonight. Your presence radiates the glory of God within each of you. Continue your passionate, loving prayers. They bring the entire heavenly choir great joy. I must depart. I am your Mother, Mary."
Scribed on 2/9/2021.

"Pain is alleviated through a sincere, contrite reconciliation with my Son. Do not delay. Make haste to purify your soul. For it

is your soul that is made in the image and likeness of God, our Father. You do not know the day nor the hour of your rendering, so be prepared. The day of atoning for your sins is always upon you. Be vigilant! Be prepared!

"Your Rosary was especially pleasing to me this evening. My crown is bursting with the bloom of new roses. Untold souls are being saved from the fires of hell at the moment of death by the holy recitation of the chaplet of divine mercy. Continue to pray it daily.

"My sons, my chosen priests, are in dire need of prayers. Pray with intense fervor that each of them live a holy, humble life of service to all my children. Pray for their liberation from any physical or spiritual attachments which encumber their lives of simplicity and virtue. Pray for an outpouring of priestly vocations. Pray for increased vocations to consecrated life. While numbers are important, nothing is more vital to the salvation of all souls than a sincere striving towards personal holiness.

"Each of you is called to personal holiness, as well. Pray and share seemingly small thoughts and words of intimacy with my Son and our Father throughout your day. Listen more, especially in adoration. Remember, you can adore our Father, my Son and the Holy Spirit anywhere, for God's creative presence is everywhere. He is in you and with you and for you. He is your constant companion in this life. Make choices so that you are His

when your spirit passes through the restraints of this life into the boundless glory of the next. Do not fall prey to the tricks of the evil one who lies in wait to capture your soul for all eternity.

"I love you and thank you for your constancy and vigilance with this prayer cenacle, especially those who were instrumental in its formation. Each day of prayer brings you immeasurable graces from the Sacred Heart of my Son, Jesus.

"Live a life of joyful thanksgiving! I know your needs. I know the desires of your heart that you murmur in the dark of night. I see your fear and anxiety. I hear your whispered pleas. I count every tear. Remember, all this will soon pass as you are joyfully welcomed to the heavenly abode.

"Go in peace. Know that you are sheltered under my mantle. My presence is the evidence of my limitless love for each of you. I am and will always be, your Mother, Mary."

Scribed on February 10, 2021

Chapter 14

Angels Among Us

Have you ever encountered someone special who has gone out of their way to bring you joy? Maybe it is a greeter at a place of business or worship. Do you smile back? Do you appreciate the effort? Or do you harden your heart with indifference, scowl, or roll your eyes? I have seen many grumpy and angry people walking this Earth with disdain for kindness and joy. They have hardened their hearts.

"I have told you this so that my joy may be in you and your joy may be complete. This is my commandment: love one another as I love you." (John 15:11-13)

During the COVID-19 pandemic and before vaccinations were available, rigid restrictions were put in place at the doctors' offices to protect the patients and staff. Everyone entering the buildings needed a temperature check and was asked the standard questions to screen for COVID-19 symptoms. This process caused extra wait time to see the doctor, and many patients grew impatient.

The nurse assigned to this task was always at a higher risk of encountering a COVID-19 patient and being exposed to this deadly virus. It was a job I would not want to do, and I always appreciated the nurse doing it.

Bette was the nurse assigned this job at the medical building we visited often. She had a beautiful smile and a kind heart. She always greeted us with joy and kindness. We could not help but smile while listening to her sweet voice and cheerful message. She always greeted me with a *"Hello, beautiful!"*

After screening us with the usual questions, she would hand me and my husband a *"Hall Pass!"* This note verified that we had been screened. Most patients were senior citizens like us; for one brief moment, she transcended us all back to high school. It made me smile. She never hesitated to say, *"God bless you!"* She was a special angel on Earth to bring cheer at a time when we lived in fear and uncertainty.

At Easter time, she dressed as the Easter Bunny. Her extra effort to make people smile was inspiring. On the *"Hall Pass,"* she wrote, *"He is risen, alleluia!"* I asked her if anyone had complained about her faith proclamation in the secular medical building. Her comment surprised me. She said that no one minded the Easter statement, but someone complained about her bunny costume! She wasn't looking for a compliment for her extra efforts, but she never expected a complaint.

Why do some people harden their hearts to one another? Why will some people spread negativity instead of love and joy? If you are unhappy right now, take time to examine the reason why. Ask the Holy Spirit to give you peace if you have no control over the reasons that make you unhappy. But if you are angry over a broken relationship or problem that you can fix, then today might be the day to do it.

"Have nothing to do with foolish, ignorant controversies; you know that they breed quarrels. And the Lord's servant must not be quarrelsome but kind to everyone, able to teach, patiently enduring evil, correcting his opponents with gentleness. God may perhaps grant them repentance leading to a knowledge of the truth, and they may come to their senses and escape from the snare of the devil after being captured by him to do his will." (Timothy 2:24-26 ESV-CE)

Chapter 15

Mary Undoer of Knots

Do you get frustrated when things do not go according to your plans? Do you get easily frustrated and feel that sometimes you feel like your shoelaces are tied in knots, and everything you try to do and every step you try to take does not work? Do you get angry? Cry? Engage in a pity party? Scream? I know I have experienced all those feelings. It is very humbling when you finally realize that we all need God's grace in our day-to-day living. Take a minute to think about a time when you were frustrated to tears, or you lost your temper. What did you do to correct the situation? Did you pray? Did you call out to God and ask for help?

I have had my share of difficult situations. The ones that always cause me the most frustration are medical problems. Since I have no medical expertise, I always feel helpless regarding anything medical-related. Unfortunately, my husband has had more than his share of medical problems and procedures. Since he is deaf in one ear, all messages and phone calls are filtered through me. His doctor wanted John to get blood work and a nuclear MRI. The technician at the MRI lab needed additional medical information that I did not have and could not provide. I contacted the medical office with the information and asked them to send it to the MRI technician in a voice message. A week later, I was informed that nothing had been done. I then contacted my husband's primary care doctor and asked for their assistance. The nurse informed me that the information I needed was embedded in a forty-four-page document and would take time to locate. Another week passed, and still no results. My frustration level was rising. In my desire to complete some of the doctor's requests, I told my husband that he needed blood work and that we would be going to the lab on Thursday morning. After reminding him not to eat since he needed to fast, I took a shower and got ready. Unfortunately, when I entered the kitchen to get my purse, I found my husband eating breakfast. Naturally, I became upset. His defense was that his short-term memory loss caused him to forget, and he was following his daily routine. My frustration was compounded by my inability to get anything done from the list of requests from the doctor. I allowed myself to have a pity party and told myself I was justified.

Later that morning, I felt a strong urge to start the Novena to Mary Undoer of Knots. Pope Francis encouraged us to rely on the Blessed Mother to untie the knots in our lives. I received an email from: PrayMoreNovenas.com with this beautiful prayer.

"In the name of the father, and of the Son, and of the Holy Spirit. Amen.

"Meditating Mother, Queen of Heaven, in whose hands the treasures of the King are found, turn your merciful eyes upon me today. I entrust into your holy hands this knot in my life [mention your request here] and all the rancor and resentment it has caused in me.

"Mary, Undoer of Knots, pray for me.

"Virgin Mary, Mother of fair love, Mother who never refuses to come to the aid of a child in need, Mother whose hands never cease to serve your beloved children because they are moved by the divine love and immense mercy that exist in your heart, cast your compassionate eyes upon me and see the snarl of knots that exists in my life. You know very well how desperate I am, my pain, and how I am bound by these knots. Mary, Mother to whom God entrusted the undoing of the knots in the lives of his children, I entrust into your hands the ribbon of my life. No one, not even the evil one himself, can take it away from your precious care. In your hands, there is no knot that cannot be undone. Powerful Mother, by your grace and intercessory power with Your Son and My Liberator, Jesus, take into your hands today this knot.

[Mention your request here]

"I beg you to undo it for the glory of God, once for all. You are my hope. O my Lady, you are the only consolation God gives

me, the fortification of my feeble strength, the enrichment of my destitution, and, with Christ, the freedom from my chains. Hear my plea. Keep me, guide me, protect me, o safe refuge! Mary, Undoer of Knots, pray for me. Amen.

"In the name of the father, and of the Son, and of the Holy Spirit. Amen."

That night in our Divine Mercy Cenacle, I was assigned St. Faustina's Diary reading 1488:

> **MY CHILD, KNOW THAT THE GREATEST OBSTACLES TO HOLINESS ARE DISCOURAGEMENT AND AN EXAGGERATED ANXIETY. THESE WILL DEPRIVE YOU OF THE ABILITY TO PRACTICE VIRTUE. ALL TEMPTATIONS UNITED TOGETHER OUGHT NOT DISTURB YOUR INTERIOR PEACE, NOT EVEN MOMENTARILY.**
>
> **SENSITIVENESS AND DISCOURAGEMENT ARE THE FRUITS OF SELF-LOVE. YOU SHOULD NOT BECOME DISCOURAGED BUT STRIVE TO MAKE MY LOVE REIGN IN PLACE OF YOUR SELF-LOVE. HAVE CONFIDENCE, MY CHILD. DO NOT LOSE HEART IN COMING FOR PARDON, FOR I AM ALWAYS READY TO FORGIVE YOU. AS OFTEN AS YOU BEG FOR IT, YOU GLORIFY MY MERCY.**

Wow! Being sensitive and discouraged are prideful and self-love. I had never looked at it that way. No longer could I feel justified.

The following day, I tried again to get John to the lab for blood work. Our morning was completely open, and I suggested we go to a restaurant for breakfast afterward. When we arrived at the lab closest to our home, we were informed that it was closed for the day due to an unexpected circumstance. We were directed to another lab on the other side of town. This lab was next to the doctor's office with the information we needed to give the MRI technician. After John gave blood, I suggested we walk next door and speak directly to someone at the doctor's office who could help us. The receptionist was accommodating and made a few calls on our behalf. Once she got the needed information to the MRI technician, she asked if we wanted to schedule the MRI for the next day! We walked away, knowing that all the frustrating obstacles had been removed. None of this would have happened if we had done blood work the day before. Sometimes roadblocks happen for a reason. If we are open to hearing His word and messages, God can help deepen our faith and guide us in His will. God knew I had received His message on sensitivity and discouragement, and Mary untied my knots. I could have stayed angry, hardened my heart, and never felt the joy of having my prayers answered, but I did not. Praise God!

Chapter 16

Trusting God (2020)

Do you turn to our God when you need help and guidance? Are you anxious about things in this world? Do world events, politics, and other things scare you and cause panic?

Whenever I turn on the news, I am confronted with chaos, disasters, violence, and corruption. The networks do not want you to change the channel, so they sensationalize the news making small events look like significant catastrophes. I find my stomach knots, and I become anxious and possibly angry. Is this how you want to live? Is this how Jesus wants us to live?

Psalm 97:12 says, "*Be glad and give thanks.*" St. Faustina tells us to trust in Jesus.

Are we truly living our faith when we allow despair and anger to consume us? Turn off the television. Read Holy Scripture instead and pray. Give God all your worries. Allow Him in your life. To truly trust in Jesus, you must believe He has a beautiful plan for your life, so thank Him. Give God thanks and praise in all things! He loves you so much! He wants you to be happy and not stressed. So "*Be glad and give thanks*" (Psalm 97:12) Jesus, I trust in you!

So much depends on the spiritual meaning of the little word "trust." Jeremiah the prophet laid it out as starkly and simply as possible: "Cursed is the man who trusts in human beings, who makes flesh his strength, whose heart turns away from the Lord." And conversely, "Blessed are those who trust in the Lord, the Lord will be their trust."

What does it mean to trust, to turn one's heart to God? It means to root the whole of one's life in God, and not to ground our concerns in the things of this world: wealth, power, pleasure, and honor.

Ask yourself: "What is the center of gravity in my life?" The Bible consistently proposes this question. For example, read the book of Joshua, when Joshua lays it on the line for the people of Israel: "Do you serve the Lord or some other gods?" That's the question being asked of you today. – Bishop Robert Barron

For St. Therese, prayer was a way of walking with God.

And it can be like this for us all.

Even in prayer, St. Therese teaches simplicity – talking to God in direct, personal, and heartfelt ways.

She prayed from her heart as a child speaks honestly and trustingly to a parent they love.

"Today, let's pray for free and open communication within our lives. Communication is the foundation to trust, honesty, and therefore love. Let's pray for this to manifest itself in our relationship with the Lord as well as in our relationships with our families and friends.

"In the name of the father, and of the Son, and of the Holy Spirit. Amen.

"Dearest Saint Therese of Lisieux, you said that you would spend your time in heaven doing good on Earth.

"Your trust in God was complete. Pray that He may increase my trust in His goodness and mercy as I ask for the following petitions...

(State your intentions)

"Pray for me that I, like you, may have great and innocent confidence in the loving promises of our God. Pray that I may live my life in union with God's plan for me and one day see the Face of God whom you loved so deeply.

"Saint Therese, you were faithful to God even unto the moment of your death. Pray for me that I may be faithful to our loving God. May my life bring peace and love to the world through faithful endurance in love for God, our savior.

"Loving God, you gave St. Therese the ability to see You in the ordinary routine of each day. Help me to be aware of your presence in the everyday events of my life.

"I see you, Lord. Help me to see you more!

"I trust you, Lord. Help me to trust you more!

"I love you, Lord. Help me to love you more!

"Glory be to the Father, to the Son, and to the Holy Spirit. As it was in the beginning, is now, and ever shall be, world without end. Amen.

"In the name of the father, and of the Son, and of the Holy Spirit. Amen.

(John-Paul & Annie - Praymorenovenas.com)

Chapter 17
Judgment Day

"We know neither the hour nor the day...." We are told to be on watch, yet death always surprises us. We are never ready to let go completely. Are you ready to die? It's a somber thought but one worth thinking about. The statistics are staggering on how many people die each day. You don't have to look far to see the senseless murders happening in our schools, stores, movie theaters, and almost everywhere, including our churches and places of worship. So, are we ready?

How will we be judged? In Matthew 25:31-46, Jesus explains the judgment of the nations. Jesus tells us we need to see Him in every person we encounter and treat them as we would Him. He also sums up what we are called to do in Matthew 22:36-39 and John 13:34-35. *"A new commandment I give to you, that you love one another: just as I have loved you, you also are to love one another. By this all people will know that you are my disciples, if you have love for one another."* (John 13:34-35)

I believe on Judgment Day we will be asked how well did we love? How well did we love God, and how well did we love one another? It's all about love! Sounds simple, but is it?

How well do you love God? Do you adore Him? Do you praise Him? Do you pray to Him daily? Is God invited into your life? God gave us free will, so it would be our choice to love Him. Have you chosen God? Do you have a relationship with Him? If not, why not? If Heaven or Paradise is being in the presence of God, and hell is the absence of God, shouldn't we want Heaven on Earth? Do we really want to wait until it's too late? *"Lord. Lord, open the door for us! But he said in reply, 'Amen, I say to you, I do not know you.' Therefore, stay awake, for you know neither the day nor the hour."*(Matthew 25:11-13) Shouldn't we want our eulogy to be, *"He/she knew Jesus?"*

Adoration and worship happen at Mass when you are in the Real Presence of Jesus at the Consecration or in front of the Monstrance with the Eucharist in Adoration. How much time do you spend with the Lord? Can you sit for an hour? Why or why not? Are you attending Mass every week? Do you go to Eucharistic Adoration? If your church doesn't offer Eucharistic Adoration, many places have perpetual adoration streaming online. Check out these sites: www.ourladyofsorrows.com, https://www.ewtn.com, and http://savior.org

Next time you have trouble sleeping, go online and pray in the Real Presence of Christ in the Eucharist when visible on the altar. It's powerful! Give Christ your worries and fears, and He will give you a good night's sleep.

How do we love one another? God's love is *agape* love: willing the good of the other. It is wanting the best for each other. If we all had *agape* love for one another, there would be no hate, gossip, jealousy, or hardened hearts. We would be the best version of ourselves.

Galatians 6:2 says, *"Bear one another's burdens, and so fulfill the law of Christ."* How do we bear one another's burdens? Do we lift people up? Or do we kick them when they are down? Does someone's misfortune make us happy, or do we reach out and help? Sometimes all it takes to brighten a person's day is a sincere compliment, a phone call, an offer to drive a neighbor to the store, a visit, a meal, and so much more. Do you have an elderly neighbor who lives alone? When was the last time you checked on them? Do you have family members you need to reconcile with and mend wounds? Please pick up the phone and call them. Life is short. On your last day, I can promise you will not wish you had spent more time at work unless you are trying to cure cancer. Instead, you will wish you spent more time with family and friends. Please do it now!

Imagine a world where we all looked out for each other and shared our food, clothing, and shelter with those who have none. Instead of complaining, fighting, hurting, and dividing, we could compliment, help, comfort, and love one another. Eutopia? I think it is Heaven on Earth. We may not be able to achieve that here, but we can try, especially in our homes and neighborhoods. If everyone reading this made a conscientious effort to put God first, humble themselves, and be an instrument of God's love, we could change the world.

One kind gesture's ripple effect is not always known, but God sees all. He knows that your kindness will cause other actions either by the person receiving the kindness or by the witnesses observing what you are doing. Our children and grandchildren are always watching. They repeat the actions that we model. Wouldn't it be nice if they copied your acts of kindness and love instead of repeating your words of anger and hate?

What will be your legacy? How will people remember you? On your last day, will you pass the test? The question will be a simple one. *"How well did you love?"* Let us not harden our hearts. Let us surrender to God and to love.

"Come, let us sing joyfully to the Lord.
Cry out to the rock of our salvation.
Let us come before him with a song of praise,
Joyfully sing out our psalms.
For the Lord is the great God,
The great king over all gods,
Whose hand holds the depths of the Earth,
Who owns the tops of the mountains.

The sea and dry land belong to God,
Who made them, formed them by hand.
Enter, let us bow down in worship.
Let us kneel before the Lord who made us.
For he is our God,
We are the people he shepherds,
The sheep in his hands.
Oh, that today you would hear his voice.
Do not harden your hearts" (Psalm 95:1-8)

Appendix

Interior Locutions During Praying of the Rosary

(These are interior locutions from the same anonymous woman in Chapter 13)

"My beloved daughters of our Most High God, the author of all life, embrace each other with loving thoughts and prayers. Remember that as you pray, once you ask my Son for a specific request, leave it with Him to do with as He wills and as our Father wills. Begging, pleading, and making unreasonable promises or trades to our Lord is an abomination. You cannot barter with our Father. He knows your every need. Make your plea plainly and with reverence and leave the rest to God. My Son and I know how to bestow sufficient graces upon you and others to sustain each of you during difficult times.

"Suffering is a purgative opportunity. Many saints in heaven gained their crowns by being sanctified in suffering. Others have offered to become victim souls for mankind. So, whatever crosses come your way, choose to carry them with simplicity and joy in silent acceptance of God's will for your life. Carry your crosses with the same humble endurance as my Son, knowing that even He fell three times on the way to Calvary. Seek your strength in silent adoration and the Bread of Life, which will always sustain

you. The Bread of Life is my Son.

"I am the spouse of the Holy Spirit and the wife of St. Joseph. The Holy Spirit is your greatest Advocate. He is the living word of my Son--the inspiration for all the gifts. The gifts flow forth from the unitive love of the Father and my Son, which are available to those who are attuned to the charisms of the Spirit. Pray worthily to receive such gifts. Our Father has chosen different gifts for different people and purposes. The gifts are especially abundant now for the remnant church. Listen for the wind, for the Spirit comes in the wind.

"Daughters, do not worry about the condition of the world--focus on the condition of your soul--and those children our Father entrusted to you. Do not fret if your children have strayed. Continue to pray and suffer for their re-conversion. Do not allow your children to think for one moment that you doubt that our Lord is their shepherd. He will not lose his own children. Their hearts are already turning more and more toward the remembered joys of their youth and my Son because of their own dismay at what the world offers. Continue to lovingly correct, lead and encourage the return of all the lost sheep. Each is precious in our Father's eyes.

"Your prayers are not only dear to me, but more importantly, to our Father and my Son. Roses now adorn the crown of my head from the Rosary you have prayed. Work diligently to overcome

fatigue in your prayer life. It is a tactic of the evil one to distract you from your prayers and faithfulness to the Trinity. You are infuriating him and his evil companions when you remain with this cenacle. You are granted sufficient strength for this day and this is a most worthy task. Thank you for your presence in person and in thought tonight for those who could not attend. I know the faithful among you. Be diligent in this effort. Now is not the time to stop. The world needs your prayers tonight and every night. I may not always be heard by one of yours, but I am always present and have been present each of the past 300 nights.

"Continue to be holy. Seek the narrow way. My Son's light will illuminate your conscience to find His path laid out for you. The more you focus on His Word, the brighter the illumination of light.

"I am Mary, Mother of Jesus, Spouse of the Holy Spirit, wife of Joseph. Stay at peace. Rest well."

Scribed on February 12, 2021

"My cherished children,

"It is I, Mary, your Mother. My Son, Jesus, and I, thank you for your continued, prayerful presence. As you pray in earnest, reflect interiorly upon your dearest requests, those closest to your heart. Then, raise your heart and mind to my beloved Son imploring his gracious indulgence in your every need and thanking him for granting the desires of your heart. He will hear

and answer each prayer in conformity with the will of His Father for what is best for each person's life. For those who are desperately ill and are frightened of death, do not fear. Remember, death is an answer to prayer, too. You do not decide the number of breaths that each person draws—that was decided by the Father himself before all of creation. This was done in union with the Son and the Holy Spirit.

"The season of fasting and penance will soon be upon you. More and more will be expected of you. Be willing to surrender every temptation and every desire to the will of our Father. He has a plan and purpose for your life and will use your silent suffering to draw you closer to His Son, Jesus. Some of you will feel as though you are experiencing your own Passion at times. Offer it willingly to our Lord in reparation for the blasphemy and sacrileges of His Most Sacred Heart. My Son will not ask of you what you cannot endure or what you will not accept.

"When you hunger, feast on my Son's Eucharistic Presence during adoration and on His Most Precious Body and Blood during Mass. Those sacraments are more than sufficient to satiate every desire. When temptation assails you, take a walk along the Way of the Cross. You may do so mentally or physically at church. These are the glories that my Son has fashioned and provided just for you. They are on the narrow way. When you partake of them, you are walking closer toward the narrow gate.

"When you reflect upon my Son's life, remember only one week was truly sorrowful and excruciatingly painful for him, but he bore it all courageously for you. While my heart was pierced seven times, His was pierced only once. Yet, you could never compare my emotional pain with His physical and emotional pain beginning in the Garden of Gethsemane. Pain is not quantifiable between two people. It is only quantifiable by the person experiencing the pain, who can only measure it against past pain. The rest of the days of my Son's life were, for the most part, days of joy and fulfillment as He shared with all the gospel of perfect Love. He is perfect Love.

"You are my chosen children and those of my Son, so live a life always striving towards perfect love. As you do, your faults diminish, and ultimately, you will arrive in the arms of Perfect Love. Become bearers of perfect love to all whom you encounter. When you fail, repent, go to Reconciliation, make amends, and start again. Do not dwell on the past, as those failings have been forgiven. You are living in the precious present moment. It is all He has given you. You have entrusted your future to His Father, so focus only upon this very moment, and all will be well. You will endure.

"I leave you tonight with the confident knowledge that your faith, hope and charity are ever-increasing. Remain faithful in prayer always."

Scribed on February 13, 2021

Feast of Our Lady of Confidence

"Oh, my cherished children of the Most High God, it is I, your Mother Mary. As you celebrate this day set aside for lovers, remember the greatest Lover of all time--the Trinity. The Father created you in His image--an image of pure Love. Your salvation was made possible by the merits of my Son's incredible sacrificial gift of His life for the love of you that you might share eternal happiness with Him. The Holy Spirit was created by the unitive love of the Father and Son, existing for all time. My Son sent you His Advocate of love to grace you with as many charisms as you need to succeed in His mission on Earth.

"The next time you attend Mass, remember all of the love that envelopes you--the love of the Father, the Son and the Holy Spirit. Also, gracing you with love are all the angels and saints in heaven as well as your own guardian angel. After Mass, linger for a little while to express your own love and thanksgiving to all those who came to shower you with love and prayers. They are worthy of your thanks and praise. Finally, I ask of you to consider offering that Mass for the person who is least deserving of your love. It is through your selfless donation of that Mass that the most hardened hearts are converted.

"My beloved daughters, over the last several nights, you have received instructions. While they are not commandments, following them will aid you on your journey toward an eternity of light and eternal joy. What is the greatest instruction? It is to continue to gather together in this cenacle, make your requests known and to pray attentively knowing that those requests are delivered to the throne of God, our Father. Be wise and do not judge anyone but yourself. Please, take heed, do not judge the merits of someone's intentions.

"Each of you have different gifts. Pray with even more conviction that your gifts will be revealed to you. Once revealed, use those gifts for the greater glory of our Father in bringing His Kingdom to Earth. You are my special daughters--bearers of HOPE--that is, bringing the light and HOPE of my Son, Jesus Christ, to a wearied and disenchanted world. Every need of yours for the particular mission entrusted to you will be provided to you. Do not abandon the tasks that our Lord has asked of each of you.

"It is the time of my departure. Know our time together is getting shorter, but it is no reflection of my love for each of you. Be at peace now, especially with each other and those within your own families.

"I am Mary, the handmaid of the Lord."

Scribed on February 14, 2021

"My beloved daughters, it is I, Mary, your Mother. Have you noticed the devastating changes taking place in your world? It is becoming harder and harder to hold back the arm of my Son, Jesus, whose justice demands retribution for the repeated offenses against His Sacred Heart and the ever-increasing belligerent blasphemies that assail our Father and wound the Trinity. Prayer has become more essential than ever.

"There are very few of you left to assuage His bleeding heart through prayers and sacrifice. Note this well, my beloved daughters who wait upon the Lord: you must serve the Lord and others with utmost joy. Anything less negates the reparation to His Sacred Heart. Pray to find your joy in serving others. Joy results in sanctity as your heart is fulfilled and you desire more and more fulfillment through good works for the Lord. As you traverse your spiritual path, subvert your own desires and pleasures and you will find the true delight of your soul--the hidden treasure of joy and union with our Lord.

"No one who ever followed our Father's will on a daily basis was deprived of true joy. In surrendering your will to the Father's, your very surrender is the first act of joy. Your surrender to our Heavenly Father must be total and complete. Hold nothing back and you will find the joy you so deeply seek.

"As you continue to discover joy in this cenacle of prayer, know that my joy is multiplied with each voice as each echoes the prayers—both vocally and mentally. Since you first gathered, you have raised innumerable bouquets of beautiful roses heavenward. It is not just fifty roses. It is fifty times each person present. You have sent a beautiful aroma heavenward that delights my senses as well as the senses of the angels and saints in Paradise. Do not stray. If you must absent yourself, pray wherever you are, and your prayers will be joined with your sisters in Christ.

"I see that your numbers are growing. There can never be too many lovely ladies serving my Son and His Father. I have chosen others to join you, but they do not yet hear the Holy Spirit calling them. They will in time. Be open to all. Be patient and diligent. Continue my invitation to all whom you encounter in this ministry.

"I leave you with JOY tonight. Be alert! I am Mary, whose soul magnifies the Lord."

Scribed on February 15, 2021

"My beloved daughters of our Most High God, King of Kings, Glory of All nations, I entreat you to seek solace in your daily habits. A life bereft of silence is a life in which there exists a barren desert. Without silence no holiness can ever water the

desert. The noisy clang of technology is drowning out the peace my Son gave to you and continues to give you in each Mass. Avoid the chaos created by chronic outbursts of noise. In noise you hear nothing. In silence, you hear everything. You may even hear the whispered voices of our Father and my Son speaking directly into your hearts. You cannot hear my voice in the clanging either. When you listen acutely in absolute silence, peace will permeate your entire being. Your heart will begin to draw closer in union with my Son. Simply slowly say with each breath, 'My Jesus, I believe, I adore, I hope, and I love You. Please pardon those who do not believe, do not adore, do not hope and do not love You' as the angel of Fatima taught my three cherished children before my appearance there. They now all occupy a special place in heaven reserved for my Son's most faithful followers.

"Pray as you go about your ordinary duties. Simply glance heavenward, acknowledge us silently and continue about your work. If you need help, ask and it will be answered. Do not let opportunities pass by during the day to seek spiritual help. We are with you every moment of every day. No request is too small or unworthy of His answer and His mercy and grace.

"I have a special request for you for tomorrow. On this day of fast and abstinence, I ask you to sit alone, quietly without notes, books, pencils, televisions, computers, cell phones or anything to

interrupt you. I ask you to think only of the first few words of the prayer that my Son taught you, the 'Our Father.' Think of 'Our Father, who art in heaven, hallowed be thy name' and with those few words on your mind, reflect on them and be drawn closer in union with the Father in prayer. Each day, take just one sentence of this prayer and meditate upon it for five minutes. It is in this way you will slowly discover the Father's divine will for you right now. Your mission may be to eliminate inappropriate language or to pray for the coming kingdom of God. Perhaps you are called to pray for the needs of the hungry this day or to pray for the conversion of souls. One of those will strike a chord in you this week and you will know what God has called you to pray for this Lent. Without meditation, there can be no fruitfulness in the spiritual path that leads to the narrow gate.

"Your prayers become more fragrant each night as your bouquet expands. Continue to be women of invitation and your flowers will carpet all of heaven. I bring special greetings of love and peace from my beloved Son, Jesus, to each of you. In His name, I send you His blessing and I give you the peace that only He can give. I leave you with His peace. I am Mary, Mother of Jesus, Son of God."

Scribed on February 16, 2021

"My beloved daughters, you form a small part of the remnant army left on Earth to pray and preserve the Body of Christ from further harm. I am your most holy Mother Mary.

"I look upon the variety of women present tonight, and I rejoice. More and more women are coming now. There is nothing that gladdens my heart more than more women praying the rosary. The surest path to heaven is through the rosary where, while meditating upon the life of my Son, Jesus, you are drawn closer to Him. This stirs in your heart a desire to spend more time with Him—in prayer, in adoration and through the reception of the sacraments He instituted. It is through the weekly reception of Reconciliation that your sins are not only forgiven, but your soul is restored to its Baptismal perfection. You also commit to avoid sin and even those behaviors that might bring you closer to sin. This sacrament of forgiveness and mercy challenges you to present yourself to Jesus in the Eucharist as blemish-free as the Passover lamb described in the Old Testament.

"Do not ever feel that your perfect heavenly Father could not possibly understand your present circumstances. He has always known them. Even so, He desires that you share every little travail with Him. Go to Him with your every need, want and desire. Nor does He expect perfection of you. Only His beloved Son, Jesus Christ, was 'perfect' in every way.

"As women of invitation, remember to ask women to join you in this beloved cenacle of prayer. You are not merely a conduit for the intentions of others, you are missionaries seeking more prayer warriors not just for this cenacle of prayer but to hasten 'His kingdom come, His will be done, on Earth as it is in heaven.' Through this avenue of prayer, the Trinity is seeking to bring all souls to perfection. I do the gathering in. My Son does the purification, which is a very necessary balm. The Holy Spirit does the rest.

"I hope and pray that the exercise on the meditation 'Our Father who art in heaven, hallowed be thy name' was a fruitful one. Our Father was pleased with those who were able to engage in this opportunity to draw closer to Him. He knows those among you who made a firm amendment to try to become more cautious in speech. This is not a failing of all, but only of some. You know who it is among you to whom this applies. Other parts of my Son's prayer to our Father apply to other warriors.

"My time is getting shorter. I may not come as often, but I am always with you. "

Scribed on February 17, 2021

"My faithful daughters, it is your holy Mother Mary. To those of you who kept a fast today and walked the stations of the cross, extraordinary graces are reserved for you. Our Father

knows how much effort you have put into this Lenten observance. You do not have to wait until Fridays to pray at the stations of the cross or meditate upon His Passion. You may do so any day of the week during Lent except Sundays because those days are not days of Lenten observance. It is better to reserve Sundays for praise, thanksgiving, and rest.

"Blessed are those among you who have come to adore my Son this week. He is very much pleased with your consistent efforts. Consistency in prayer and conversation with Him is the secret to intimate union with Him. Do not abandon Him these 40 days because of other spiritual practices. Nothing is more important than the time you spend united with him. Open your heart. Pour forth your wants, needs and desires. He is waiting to direct the Holy Spirit to give you His generous gifts.

"Each of you will face very different challenges this Lent. Fortify yourself on the Eucharist, where my Son's divine presence will accompany you throughout your day. If this is simply not possible, focus your prayers on a spiritual communion accompanied by prayers of thanksgiving and praise for His many blessings. It is not until you no longer have something that you can truly appreciate how truly blessed each of you is.

"Thank you for your faithfulness to this prayer group. Soon, each of you will discern why you were called to this cause.

"I must depart now, but I shall return for a brief while."

Scribed on February 19, 2021

"I am the Queen of Heaven, your Blessed Mother Mary. I am overjoyed with the constancy and consistency of the days of your prayers, especially of the rosary. The rosary in these dark times will remain your greatest spiritual weapon against the evil one. Avoid the evil one by never engaging with him. He is far more persuasive than you and is filled with such trickery and deceit that he could never be conquered without your armor of sacraments, grace, and prayers. So, continue to fortify yourselves. Frequently receive the Sacrament of Reconciliation. Receive ever more frequent my Beloved Son's gift of Himself—the Eucharist. Pray, pray, pray! Grace will be abundant.

"Despite the sin and evil that abounds in your world, seek those who are doing the will of the Father. These are the ordinary people—grandparents, parents, adults, youth and even the children who are engaged in their daily work but are doing it all for the glory of God, the Father. They are not self-seeking. They are models of humility and charity. They are proponents of peace in all aspects of their lives. They accept their trials with grace and understanding of how much they are loved by the Father and my Son. Those who are tried by the fire of suffering on this Earth will

enjoy the perfection of heaven in all its splendor and glory. Do not resist your trials. They purify you!

"Do not judge one another. You truly do not know what each is enduring. Some will share their circumstances and others will not. There is no harm in seeking prayer for your situation—it is encouraged. It is not the ease of this life that determines the destiny of one's soul for eternal life. Keep your eyes focused on the eternity of your soul for it will endure forever. Its destination is your utmost concern."

Scribed on February 20, 2021

"Daughters of the Most High King of All Glory,

"It is I, Mary Immaculate, who has come to beseech you to ask my Son, to be your personal companion and guide. He is already your personal Savior. So many of you feel at an interior level that you do not have a personal relationship with my Son. I assure you, each of you has had a unique personal experience where my only beloved Son, Jesus, has touched your life in otherwise inexplicable ways. If I held each you accountable at this very moment to share the one time you were absolutely certain of the existence of God, the Father, the Son or the Holy Spirit, each would be able to relate such an experience. The cornerstone of

your faith, the belief in the existence of the Trinity would be palpable.

"Call upon your guardian angel as well as St. Michael, the Archangel, protector of the Church and guardian of all souls, to inspire you with all the attributes you seek to perfect your own soul. He was the consummate model of humility, courage and strength. Call upon him as you wage war against the enemy. He will give you his strength and courage to overcome temptation and sin, especially repetitive sin.

"Many of you have asked me in prayer to reveal your most offensive sin so that you may remedy your ways before the hour of your death. I tell you now the most offensive sin is blasphemy—blasphemy against the Holy Names of God, the Father, My Most Precious Son and against the Holy Spirit. The second is the one that you will not give up—the one you continue to confess each at each sacramental Reconciliation. Focus on remedying those two and you will bring great joy to the Trinity and the heavenly choir of angels and saints.

"Each of you has made great progress on your spiritual journey. Although you did not know I saw you on Day 1 and I have seen how much your heart seeks to discover the needs of others. This is a particular joy for me. I am praying for each of you now and I have been praying for you each "now" that has elapsed since this cenacle of prayer began. I was there in that

"now," which is now "then." Did you feel my maternal presence? I was the one encouraging you, assuring you and my graces were giving you increased doses of fortitude and piety.

"I see how reverently and worthily you receive my beloved Son in the Sacrament of the Eucharist. I have noticed the sincerity of your heart. Do not ever forget to offer My Son's Body and Blood for your own personal intention. At that precise moment, you are in perfect union with Christ Himself—He has and is making Himself fully available only to you in that moment. Do not waste another communion with our Lord, Jesus.

"It has not gone unnoticed that more of you are lingering after Mass to spend a few moments with my Son. This is the highest honor you can bestow upon Him—a truly, sincere thanksgiving for Him giving His life so that you can spend an eternity with Him. How beautiful you are together!

"It is with great joy that I greeted you and it is with some urgency that I depart. It would be remiss of me to take flight without assuring you that the Holy Spirit has already been sending you gifts quite generously. Some of you are starting to hear our voices but have doubts. To you, I offer these words of encouragement. Pick up your writing implement and simply write what you think you hear. You are only putting them in the privacy of your prayer journal. After a while you may wish to share your

journal an intimate friend like my Son Jesus. Always test the voices you hear. The devil loves to disguise himself as one of us.

"The gifts of the spirit are not alien. They are over 2,000 years known to all. Embrace the Holy Spirit, your Advocate. He was the final gift from my Son to you—but the Spirit is not the final gift—the Spirit comes in the wind bearing gifts. Do not reject my Son's most generous gift to you before His death. The Spirit truly keeps giving. It is the nature of the Holy Spirit, the giver of the gifts.

"I must be about my Father's business. Goodnight. I am Mary, under the mantle of Our Lord."

Scribed on February 22, 2021

"My beloved children,

"It is so amazing to see you gathered here tonight with expectant hope, uplifted hearts, and sincerity of prayer. Each day you become more and more precious to me as each decade of the rosary is prayed with sincerity and grace. As you pray, remember, it is the life of my beloved Son who is the focus of your attention and desire. Pray and meditate upon each mystery with deliberation and care. Ask our Lord to reveal Himself more perfectly to you each night. If asked, He will do so. He only desires to capture your heart and soul for all eternity. They [your heart

and soul] were the Father's in the beginning. Make sure they are His for an eternity.

"Continue your sacramental participation frequently attending to the condition of your soul. Most worthily receive the Body and Blood of my beloved Son poured out daily on every altar of the world. Receive Him reverently and then all of His amazing humanity and perhaps a bit of His divinity will be brought to fruition in you. Rest in Him. Love Him. Adore Him. Do not ever lose hope or despair of your circumstances. Your trials are perfecting you.

"As you pray your beautiful rosaries, remember the cardinal virtues of faith, hope and charity are becoming ever more abundant in you. Your faith was a gift to you. Unless you unwrap the gift and continue to explore its increasing intricacies, it will be like the first blossom of a flower never brought to full bloom – Beautiful to observe, but without any depth. You mortals love acronyms and one of you wrote that H. O. P. E. means How Our Problems End. That is only an absolute truth if that truth is rooted in the HOPE of my beloved Son, Jesus. As you are well aware, the perfection of charity is the greatest of all the virtues. My Son is the perfection of charity and so is the Father. The Father "so loved the world that He gave you His only beloved Son so that whoever believes in Him should not perish but have eternal life. This "gift giver" – our great and generous Father – is the epitome

of charity, often overlooked. How gracious, how good, how perfect is our Father!

"My children, you have seen your loved ones suffer. Imagine the depth of our Father's love for you that He would sacrifice His only Son just so you could spend an eternity with the Father, the Son and the Holy Spirit. Your tender hearts abhor suffering. Yet the Father gave his Son without sparing Him any Earthly suffering. Now do you have a sense of the measure of the depth of His love for you? Love generously.

"My daughters, each of you is precious in my sight. Shine with the glory with which God surrounds you regardless of the circumstances of your life. Do not be distressed about any matter – large or small. If you feel yourself falling – worry not. You are only falling into the arms of Jesus. You will be cradled with love. My mantle of security and serenity will help blanket your rest. Then, rise to face your challenges. Let the glory of the Lord envelop you. Rest only in Him.

I am your Mother Mary, Consoler of All.

Scribed on February 23, 2021

My beloved daughters of the Mighty and Most Glorious King of Heaven and Earth,

"'O sing to the Lord a new song; sing to the Lord, all the Earth!' As King David sang with timbrel and harp, '[B]less His

name; tell of His salvation from day to day, Declare his glory among nations, His marvelous works among all the peoples! For great is the Lord, and greatly to be praised; He is to be feared above all gods.'

"And, so, my children, I say to each one of you tonight, Pray in glory! Let glory shine all about you! Say to all: 'The Lord reigns.' These are the very words I, too, sang as a young girl. There is one line of this joy-filled psalm to which many pay no attention. To you, I say, take heed. 'Worship the Lord in holy attire.' [Psalm 96: I-9]

"My beloved, your children and the next generation scream out that it is 'enough' for our Lord if they just 'show up' to the celebration of the Eucharist. They complain that what they wear and whether they are participating matters not. Listen acutely to the admonition. Each of you is to bring GLORY to His name, bring an offering, wearing holy attire when worshiping the Lord. Ah, my child, you ask: What is holy attire? It is not the wealth of the finery upon your body but rather the sacredness of it. Do your clothes bring glory to our Father or admonition? Do your clothes call for a blessing upon you? Are they seeking only the divine without a call for personal attention? These are the questions you are to instruct your children and your grandchildren to ask of themselves. They are simply questions. They are your judgments, but they allow your dear, precious

family to understand what it is that our Father asks of those who seek to hallow Him and bring glory upon Him. It answers the question, 'May I come as I am dressed?'

"Do not confuse the psalmist's message with the very, very different question of 'Do I come as I am?' Yes, you most definitely do come exactly as you are and my beloved Son, Jesus, will meet you exactly where you are. He will embrace you with mercy and joy. His arms will be around you as you walk through the door and search for your pew. He will be with you from the moment of your arrival to the moment of your last departure. Your guardian angel will also accompany you bearing your offering to the Lord. Make sure that the offering plate is filled with your good deeds from a joyful heart. Come and be filled with the joy of the Lord as you praise and sing of His great and mighty deeds.

"This cenacle of prayer is almost liturgical in its expression of words. Contemplate this. You gather together each night and make your requests plainly known to the Lord. You actively and joyfully voice statements of praise and thanksgiving for all known answered prayer. Thus, your prayers of thanksgiving are a song unto the Lord, a beautiful harmony of diverse voices brought together by invitation. Once you have made your requests known, rest in the certain knowledge that our Lord and Savior, my Son, Jesus Christ, has heard these requests as has our Father. Those requests in consonance with the Father's will are

granted. Continue to gather and pray. It is the prayer and the multiplicity of voices that are a new song unto our Lord. Never is there a night it seems when one person has the exact same prayer task or assignment. It is this variability of tenor that brings a beautiful explosion of euphonies to the heavenly hosts and opens the throne room of Heaven. You are a beautiful delight unto our Lord!

"With joy in your heart, sing, praise Him and make your pleas known to him. Your faithfulness to this cenacle will be rewarded with grace upon grace. You shall dance in the dawn of eternal light as you pass through the narrow gate. Remain faithful and sincere.

"I am Mary, the handmaid of the Lord, who has been magnified by Him for all generations."

Scribed on February 24, 2021

"Oh, most cherished children chosen from an eternity to be here tonight, it is I, Mary, your humble servant and the spouse of St. Joseph. I look lovingly upon you this beautiful evening, hopeful that each of you will forever remain faithful to the commands of the Father not only today but all the days of your lives.

"Here is a solution central to a challenge many of you still face: live a life of deliberate simplicity. So many of you, my precious daughters, have unnecessarily complicated your lives by

the accumulation of material goods, excessive food presentations and complicated interpersonal relationships. Focus upon those whom the Father put on your path today. You need not venture any further. You were not born to save the world. My Son was already born. He was crucified, died, buried and rose, again, so that you would inherit eternal life. His life-giving task will never be your life-altering task.

"Perhaps you might consider beginning your day of prayer with your imminent death upon your mind—not in a frightening or foreboding manner—but with the full realization that all you have on this Earth will be left behind. Only your soul will ascend to the Father for judgment. So, build a treasury of spiritual works of kindness—first to your spouse. Secondly, speak with love and clarity with your adult children. Never confuse the minds and expectations of your children. If your entire life is spent in the bubble of your family—you will have traveled very far IF you have treated each ember as you would have treated my own beloved Son. They were each created by the Father. He loves each of them as much as He loved His beloved Son, Jesus Christ. God also loves you incalculably. So, speak with gentleness of tongue, but with clarity of vision. The only treasure worth gaining is to rest forever in the arms of Jesus under His Father's eternal gaze.

"Put aside past hurts or bitterness. Entrust those to me. I am here with you now in this moment. Our God and Father will be

kind and merciful with your past sins as long as you have lived your present life according to the sacraments—those grace-filled personal encounters with Jesus—and according to the Father's commandments—those rubrics of morality. Frequent the sacraments daily, if possible. When not possible, linger longer in prayer and thanksgiving.

"Children, you can always retreat to the desert of your heart and mind. Go there when distracted or distressed—even if only to quiet yourself and in doing so, you will quiet your soul. While my Son lay dying, thrust upon the cross of horror and humiliation, I could only remain at the foot of that cross by retreating to the desert of my heart and mind for brief moments. There I found great joy and consolation I the promise of His Resurrection. There, I found solace in remembered joy. In this way you, too, will always avoid a spirit of discouragement.

"I am grateful for your loyalty and fidelity to these prayers and to this cenacle. Roses and their sweet aroma are filling the heavenly realm. I am your Blessed Mother of the Heavenly Host. I come always with peace in my heart and upon my lips. I serve the one, true, eternal God—the Trinity of Father, Son and Holy Spirit.

Scribed on February 25, 2021

"O, my cherished children of God, the Father Almighty, it is I, your holy Mother Mary. I have come to tell you of richness and a

wealth of mystical experiences that await those who embrace the faithful recitation and mediation upon each mystery of the rosary. If you heed the call to come and pray, you will immediately take note that you must slow down the pace of your life to reverently recite the prayers. Your focus should never be only upon the prayers but rather upon one particular aspect of my Son's life. When you truly join My Son, Jesus, in His life, your intimate union with Him is very much strengthened. Eventually, your union will be so close that you may be able to proclaim as St. Paul that it 'is no longer I who lives, but Christ who lives in me.'

"Nurture the transformative power of the rosary. Do not reserve it solely for this group. There are times when you cannot pray with them. There are other times when there is simply no other prayer that brings you in sure and intimate union with Jesus. Then, there are those times when simply no other prayer will rise to meet your needs! Pray it all times and under all circumstances! The graces are incalculable.

"I find delight in you. Your Heavenly Father finds great joy and delight in each of you. He knew you before He knit you in your mother's womb. He knew you before He created the first man, Adam. He knew you before He created the world and separated the water from the dry lands. He knew you before time existed. He knew you, and He loved you always! You are His

delight, and each prayer—internal and vocal, increases His delight in you!

"There are so many children in your world who are growing up without their fathers, and their lives are fractured, as are their families. It is critical to pray that the kingdom of God comes to your Earth, where your spiritual Father and my espoused, St. Joseph, may lead and shelter the fatherless. He was a true and holy father to my beloved Son, Jesus, in every way except biology. This is because the Father in His perfection would only choose perfection in a human father for His only beloved Son, Jesus. Continue to implore your Heavenly Father to let His 'kingdom come, [His] will be done on Earth as it is in Heaven.' In this way, there will be a slow but powerfully palpable restoration of physical and spiritual paternity on Earth.

"During this time, you must at all times, pray in the Spirit, seeking the gift that the Father wills for your life. For what is good for one is quite disastrous for another. The Holy Spirit knows the Father's will for you. He will answer your prayers in the Father's perfect timing for your life.

"I am Mary, handmaid of the Lord, your spiritual mother and refuge. I alight with your intentions to transport and transmit them to our Father in Heaven."

Scribed on February 27, 2021

"Beloved children of the Light of Christ, I am the tabernacle of your beloved Savior, Jesus Christ. I come to you tonight to warn you that time is beginning to spiral to an end for those who desire mercy and not justice. This is my bugle call. I am sounding the alarm that you are to prepare your heart to receive my Son by purifying your soul. Run to Reconciliation. Tarry not any longer. Grab your loved ones. Take them with you. Make a complete confession of all sins—past, present, and especially repetitive. Be precise in your enumeration as is possible. Spare no detail for to spare is to sin again, and that, too, must be confessed.

"Your devotion to me is very pleasing. Be assured that my purpose is primarily directional. I point you to Jesus always. Jesus is Perfect Love. He simplified and distilled the Old Testament commandments from ten to two: (1) Love God above all else. (2) Love your neighbor as yourself. Just as Jesus forgives you in the Sacrament of Reconciliation, you are to forgive your neighbors. Who are your neighbors? Everyone who has injured you is your neighbor—all on Earth. It is not a degree of proximity. Keep uppermost in your mind that the measure you measure with will be measured against you. Avoid the measure with constant striving towards love of all.

"Present a pure heart of surrender to my beloved Son. If you do, my grace will spare you. You will be reserved for eternal life in glory with God the Father.

"Remember, time is short! Make a perfect Reconciliation as is possible for you in your present state of sin. Center your focus on the object of my desire: Jesus Christ. Strive towards perfect love of God and neighbor. This is achieved by constant forgiveness of those who have wronged you. Do not keep account of anyone's wrongs, for to forgive is to forget and begin anew.

"Time is of the essence. Make amends today. I must depart in haste. I am, as always, Mary, the Mother of Christ."

Scribed on March 1, 2021

"Children of the Price of Light, it is I, Mary, who comes to you amidst the trials and tribulations of daily life. Today was a but a minute sampling of the patience you will need to develop in order to gain the rewards of eternal life. At all times, turn and direct your gaze upon the most holy face of My Son, Jesus. In it, all the worries of your world are dissolved. Talk to Jesus as you would your best friend, for He should occupy that place in your own heart.

"Some of you would prefer to gaze upon His shoulder wound, the most serious wound of all the injuries He sustained before His heart was finally pierced. Meditate upon the wound and recount your own sinfulness. In this way, you will learn to recognize how each of you contributed to the Passion and Death of my beloved Son, Jesus Christ. No one is blameless in the eyes of God. All are

guilty of sin. Graciously, your original sins were washed away in the waters of Baptism. You have the opportunity to wash away all your other sins each time you avail yourself of the Sacrament of Reconciliation. This sacrament cleanses your entire spirit! I am aghast that it is now only recommended once a month. Can you amend your habitual sin by atoning once a month? Of course, not. Frequency, fullness, and finality are the hallmarks of an excellently confessed soul.

"The soul is taken frequently to the waters of forgiveness where they fully confess all sins committed, including the number of times each sin was committed. Each confession must be sincerely and fully made, sparing no detail. In this way, the penitent is fully and finally forgiven. Now, in this state of total and perfect grace, the soul is prepared to receive the Body and Blood, Soul and Divinity of my Most Beloved Son, Jesus Christ. How well are you prepared to receive Him?

"I leave you to ponder this question: Does Jesus occupy your heart as your very dearest friend?

"I am Mary, Queen of the Universe."

Scribed on March 2, 2021

"Ladies of the Father's Will, it is I, Mary, Consoler of All Hearts. Your time is drawing short. The world is more divisive than ever. I have come to call you to unite to the heart of my Son,

Jesus Christ, and cease all divisions among you. Your entire life is a matter of repetitive choice, that is, you make one choice after the other. No one does the choosing except you. The Father will never foist His will upon you. You control the ship as its master. Whether mercy or justice is yours is largely a matter of where you steer your choices in the prudent exercise of your free will.

"I cannot stress enough at this time the necessity of utilization of the Sacrament of Reconciliation. None of you know the day nor the hour when you will be called to render an accounting of your life. Be prepared! Every grievance against another, no matter how slight or innocuous you may deem it, shall be confessed. Hold nothing back! My Son will never deny you the need of a holy priest to whom you can confess.

"It is never for you to judge the soul or interior life of any of my sons who are consecrated to my Son. The souls of saints are often clothed in disarray and disguise. It matters not anyway as the character and reputation of the humanity of my priests do not affect their ability to appear in the person of my Son, Jesus Christ. Remember, even Judas was chosen to follow my Son. My Father does the choosing of those admitted to holy orders. Who are you to object? Leave all else to the Father, as well. Those shepherds who do not lead their flocks to Jesus will spend an eternity in the pit of hell. That is consequence enough!

"The well of forgiveness is still very deep. The waters are brimming over. Come bathe in the waters of mercy before the drought is upon you. Do not delay any longer!

"You must gather more souls in towards Jesus. Tell others of His great love for them. Explain that this life is fleeting, but eternal life is forever. The desire for Heaven must be uppermost on your minds during all your waking hours. The more you contemplate upon your permanent home, and your spiritual reward in Heaven, the greater will be your desire to strive to imitate Perfect Love—Jesus Christ.

"I longingly await the day we no longer see dimly lit but rather see each other face-to-face.

"I must take my leave. I am Mary, the Immaculate Virgin, Mother of Jesus Christ. I leave you with the overwhelming abundant graces of love and peace."

Scribed on March 3, 2021

"My beloved daughters of the Glorious King of Heaven and Earth,

"Peace be with you today and always. Keep peace among you and with all whom you encounter, especially within your family. Great saints have risen to the heights of glory by remaining silent in the face of adversity. This is not an impossible attainment. It is

made easier with offering your suffering up to God, for it is there that grace abounds.

"Remember, also, that the gifts of the Holy Spirit are graces, too—extraordinary graces. These gifts are never to be rashly requested by any of you. When you learn that God is giving certain souls extraordinary graces as was once done with the prophets, you must never ask or desire Him to give you the same gift, for this would be the sin of pride—a sin against humility. Having a gift is not a reflection of the state of the soul of the person possessing the gift. God can use any soul for his divine purpose.

"Secondly, you may very well open yourself up to a different type of spiritual warfare—opening doors that may very well allow access for the devil and his minions, which would have disastrous consequences for your soul. Remember the Words of St. Matthew, 'On that day many will say to Me "Lord, Lord, did we not prophesy in your name, and cast out demons in your name, and do many mighty works in your name? And then will I declare to them 'I never knew you; depart from me, you workers of lawlessness.' [Matt. 7: 22-23]

"Likewise, let us reflect on the gift of tongues. What use is the gift of tongues if there is no one to interpret? A person could be cursing My Son or our Father. Who would know if no one interprets? That is why only one or two should ever speak in tongues. For every speaker, there must be one to interpret.

"The path to holiness is yours with or without the extraordinary graces or gifts of the Holy Spirit. The sanctifying grace you received at Baptism and the spiritual effects of Confirmation are sufficient for you. The charismatic gifts are always gifts given for the betterment of the community in which they are given. So, if you have been given the gift of tongues and there are none to interpret or understand, be silent in the community and speak alone with God.

"When a prophet speaks, the prophecy must be judged by someone who has the knowledge to judge the prophecy. Is it from the Lord, or is it from the netherworld? Prophecy and revelation must be done one at a time. Woe to him or her who is a false prophet!

"At all times, place all your concerns before the tabernacle of my beloved Son's heart. Remain with Him in prayerful silence. He will reveal the error of your ways. He may point you in the direction of one of my holy sons to guide you on your spiritual journey. At all times and under all circumstances, remain faithful to the Church and her ministries. Do not stray from the tabernacle of the Lord, your God.

"I continue to delight in your presence and rejoice in your progress on the spiritual path prepared for you by the Father.

"I am Mary, descendant of King David, chosen to be the tabernacle for our Lord and Savior, Jesus Christ."

Scribed on March 5, 2021

"My beloved daughters of the Glorious King of Heaven and Earth,

"Peace be with you today and always. Keep peace among you and with all whom you encounter, especially within your family. Great saints have risen to the heights of glory by remaining silent in the face of adversity. This is not an impossible attainment. It is made easier with offering your suffering up to God, for it is there that grace abounds.

"Remember, also, that the gifts of the Holy Spirit are graces, too—extraordinary graces. These gifts are never to be rashly requested by any of you. When you learn that God is giving certain souls extraordinary graces as was once done with the prophets, you must never ask or desire Him to give you the same gift, for this would be the sin of pride—a sin against humility. Having a gift is not a reflection of the state of the soul of the person possessing the gift. God can use any soul for his divine purpose.

"Secondly, you may very well open yourself up to a different type of spiritual warfare—opening doors that may very well allow access for the devil and his minions, which would have disastrous consequences for your soul. Remember the Words of St. Matthew,

'On that day many will say to Me "Lord, Lord, did we not prophesy in your name, and cast out demons in your name, and do many mighty works in your name? And then will I declare to them 'I never knew you; depart from me, you workers of lawlessness.' [Matt. 7: 22-23]

"Likewise, let us reflect on the gift of tongues. What use is the gift of tongues if there is no one to interpret? A person could be cursing My Son or our Father. Who would know if no one interprets? That is why only one or two should ever speak in tongues. For every speaker, there must be one to interpret.

"The path to holiness is yours with or without the extraordinary graces or gifts of the Holy Spirit. The sanctifying grace you received at Baptism and the spiritual effects of Confirmation are sufficient for you. The charismatic gifts are always gifts given for the betterment of the community in which they are given. So, if you have been given the gift of tongues and there are none to interpret or understand, be silent in the community and speak alone with God.

"When a prophet speaks, the prophecy must be judged by someone who has the knowledge to judge the prophecy. Is it from the Lord, or is it from the netherworld? Prophecy and revelation must be done one at a time. Woe to him or her who is a false prophet!

"At all times, place all your concerns before the tabernacle of my beloved Son's heart. Remain with Him in prayerful silence. He will reveal the error of your ways. He may point you in the direction of one of my holy sons to guide you on your spiritual journey. At all times and under all circumstances, remain faithful to the Church and her ministries. Do not stray from the tabernacle of the Lord, your God.

"I continue to delight in your presence and rejoice in your progress on the spiritual path prepared for you by the Father.

"I am Mary, descendant of King David, chosen to be the tabernacle for our Lord and Savior, Jesus Christ."

Scribed on March 5, 2021

"Beloved daughters of the King of Heaven and Earth, it is I, Mary, Queen of the Universe, your sure and steady guide to the Sacred Heart of my Son, Jesus Christ.

"Seek all consolation in the Heart of Jesus, for it has known all pain. There is no distress that He was spared on Calvary, and His heart continues to bleed for all the offenses continually committed against the Father. May you make an offering of reparation for your sins as promptly as you are able.

"May the God of all kindness and mercy send His graces upon you. May you rest in the assurance that your prayers are pleasing to the King of Heaven and Earth. Continue to invoke His name as

you go about your daily tasks as He is with you always. He loves you. He delights in you. You are precious and glorious to Him. Remain steadfast in your faith. Remain diligent in prayer and study.

"I will take my leave of you tonight, knowing that each of you is making progress on the path before you. Do not compare your progress to others. Each of you must make your own spiritual journey.

"I am Mary, Mother of Jesus, Savior of All."

Scribed on March 7, 2021

"O my beloved daughters of Christ, the Crucified Son of God, Your numbers are increasing and noted. Continue to be women of invitation and prayer. Do not dread the "no" you may receive, for it is not directed to you but rather to my beloved Son, Jesus Christ, who died for all sinners and rose, again, on the third day.

"Your prayers are a delight to the Father, the Son, and the Holy Spirit, the inexplicable Trinity of God. Your voices are sweeter than a choir of angels praising, 'Holy, holy, holy, Lord God Almighty.' Continue to pray with fervent intensity for the needs of all who have asked, but do not forget to ask of those who request prayers to join with you in prayer.

"There will be many saints from the laity. Be content to pray for holy families and strengthening of the bonds of marriage. As

you well know from my message at Fatima, the family is Satan's final battleground. You know that the gates of hell will not prevail against my Son's Church. Similarly, Satan will never destroy holy families. Pray! Pray! Pray! This is my fervent intention. You have available many sacramentals to use for the benefit of lukewarm souls. Use them so that upon judgment, they will not be spit out but raised to the heavenly courts.

"Do not ever cease the prayers for my consecrated sons. Satan strives hardest to tempt them to the point of perdition. Nothing will preserve the laity greater than the sacraments administered by holy priests. Pray also that they persevere in presenting the Word of God, the traditions, and doctrines faithfully and clearly. My Son is raising up holy men to the altar of the Lord. Pray that their holiness is preserved.

"Continue to surrender everything to me. I know how to have my Son use it for the greatest glory and honor of God, the Father."

"I must alight. It is I, Mary, Mother of Jesus, under whose mantle you are secure and protected from all harm."

Scribed on March 9, 2021

"Beloved daughters of our Triune God, peace be with you.

"Have confidence, my daughters, that your requests are being made known to God the Father. He knows all, sees all, and grants each request as well bring each soul in closer union with Him.

The answer "no" can reap a great spiritual harvest by perfecting the virtues of that soul whose request was denied. In those instances where a life hangs in the balance between your world and the spiritual world, remember that God will pluck a soul from Earth and bring him to particular judgment at the moment that soul is closest to God. Your Father is a God of mercy and justice, always embracing Love itself. So, do not fret. Once you have offered your intention, your own souls should be content and find joy in knowing you have fulfilled your promise to request prayers on one's behalf.

"Prayer—conversation with the Father, Son, and Holy Spirit should bring you great consolation and JOY! So, put away your fatigue and forlorn expressions and live in the joy of loving the eternal High Priest, Jesus Christ. For you have now encountered perfect LOVE! In Him, you will find the perfect PEACE that only He can bring.

"Each of you continues to bring me great joy and delight. You have gathered many roses over the past ten or so months, which now carpet heaven. Continue to pray in this cenacle gathering with all those who desire to join you. Pray, more importantly, for the conversion of hardened hearts that they may be softened much like the prodigal Son who desired to return home to his Father. Until death occurs, it is never too late for conversion.

"Each of you is precious and glorious to the Father. Continue to walk in the way of my Son, and the glory of heaven will one day be yours. Remember each misdeed, no matter how slight, must be confessed, forgiven, and atoned for. Do not waste an opportunity for your soul to be healed.

"Grace is raining upon you as I depart. The grace of my Son, Jesus Christ, is sufficient for you today and always.

"I am Mary, cousin of Elizabeth. I, too, am a child of God, who is highly favored."

Scribed on March 10, 2021

"My beloved daughters,

"How precious, glorious and delightful you are as you pray and lift up your voices. Grace rains down like holy water on your skin tonight, just as it did at Baptism. As your faith blossoms and matures, you become more transformed into the light of Jesus Christ, my Son. Many of you now are able to lead others to Me, but I only point them to my Son. I would have no merit if it were not to direct others to Jesus. As you draw nearer to Him in prayer, I will shelter you beneath my mantle of protection.

"As you become more sensitive to the gifts God has bestowed upon you, you will see His works and the awesome deeds He has done for each of you. Then, you will sing praise to our Father God, who hears your prayers.

"Flock to the Father of Heaven and Earth in Confession. Beg of Him to pardon all your sins, for only He has the power to forgive you. Be washed clean as you were in the waters of Baptism. Then, fulfill your penance and promise to sin no more.

"Look to the heights of the mountains and the power of the raging sea. Surely, you know only a good and perfect God created these for you. Only Jesus calmed the roar of the sea and the raging, murmuring people. The same Heavenly Father who provides for you also provides the rain for the fields and sun for the plants to grow. Without the Father, the Earth would become a desolate wasteland.

"This I say to you tonight: Shout joyfully to the Lord in thanksgiving for the gifts and graces that He has bestowed upon you. Imagine, if only for a moment, that those whom you neglected to pray for or those accouterments of your life for which you never expressed gratitude were taken from you. How empty would your life be? So, sharpen your efforts of thanksgiving.

"Then, when you shout as the psalmist shouted, 'Graciously, rescue me, God! Come quickly to help me, Lord!' Your Heavenly Father, who knows what you need, will be by your side, leading you along the path of righteousness until you are safely delivered from those who seek your ruin. Do not pray in haste. Rather, in all things, pray in grateful thanksgiving for the gifts, graces, and blessings bestowed upon you as his chosen children.

"The Father, the Son, and the Holy Spirit love you with an everlasting love. They will guide you all the days of your life if you but ask. You who love the Lord, your God, with your whole heart and soul will dwell with Him for eternity."

"I bring the glory of the Father and the Son and Holy Spirit with me tonight. May you continue to seek and rejoice in the Trinity always.

"I am Mary, whose Immaculate Heart burns with the love of our Triune God. Peace be with you!"

Scribed on March 11, 2021

"Beloved daughters of the Prince of Peace,

"You are growing more precious to me each evening. As the days grow longer, I see your devotion increasing. I continue to embrace you and keep you protected under my mantle of mercy. Continue to grow in the love of my Son through this cenacle of prayer. He is most pleased with your daily recitation of the Divine Mercy Chaplet. You are casting a wide net for souls sparing them eternal damnation with this prayer and placing these souls square in the mercy of my Son and the Father. Miracles are being wrought by your faithfulness. Do not depart from these prayers.

"Make every effort to grow in virtue, especially fortitude, justice, patience, and temperance. They will serve you well throughout your life. When you have championed those, continue

to grow in faith, hope, and love. In doing so, you will triumph in finding and discerning the divine will of the Father for you. His divine will is for you to be holy and spend eternal happiness with Him.

"I am Mary, Queen of the Rosary."

Scribed on March 12, 2021

"My beloved daughters,

"Your faithfulness does not go unnoticed. It brings immense joy to me and to my beloved Son that you are here each evening. Your faith, borne out through acts of mercy and charity, coupled with faithfulness in prayer, will gain you great merit before the throne of God, our Father.

"Remember, to encourage the youth in your life to pray to our Father to assist each of them in discerning the vocation each should pursue. So many of my children go about pursuing their own desires without ever asking our Father what His divine will is for their lives. They are then left to wonder why doors are closed and chosen careers do not fulfill them. Only God, our Father, can fill their hearts, yet He is omitted from their consideration. This is a great failing in this generation. Pray that their hearts, minds, and souls will be opened to the joy to be found in a developed prayer life that is, a true relationship with my Son, Jesus Christ, and his Father in Heaven.

"Our time together is getting shorter, but I am always with you. Do not look with the eyes of this world but see with the eyes of your soul. Set your sights always on the eternal where you will encounter the divine forever and ever.

"I am Our Lady of the Rosary, who prays for you now and at the hour of your death."

Scribed on March 16, 2021

"Beloved of God the Father,

"You have been chosen from all time for the vocation you now have—prayer warrior. What your world needs now is more prayer warriors. Your beloved Father in Heaven hears not only your prayer requests, but all the requests ever made to Him. He knew them before they were ever made, ever needed, before all time. He knows all. For our Heavenly Father, all time is now in the present, for He always was, always is and always will be. So, is prayer and its necessity. Therefore, draw in as many as you can. Form additional cenacles if the group becomes unwieldy, but do not abandon the call to pray for as St. Paul instructed you—your prayers should be never ceasing.

"Your prayers do not need be formulaic all day long as though you were a single contemplative woman dedicated to a life of prayer and fasting, rather there are other ways to have an entire day of prayer and still accomplish what other tasks have been set

before you. As you awaken and praise our Lord and God for another day of breath and health, seek out the Father's will for you that day. Seek to know His will and do His will. Then, dedicate your day and hours for different intentions. As you move throughout your day, simply raise your eyes to heaven silently remembering your request. Then, go about your daily activities doing all to best of your abilities and all for the greater glory of God. Whatever is set before you, simply do it with joy as if the granting of the intention was dependent on the quality of your work.

"As your day draws to a close, you will discover that you have lived a very joy-filled, joyful, and productive day advancing ever nearer the narrow gate and growing more and more in holiness. If you have erred, seek my Son's forgiveness and begin anew each day. You may also offer your trials as a form of prayer—loneliness, sadness, disappointment, boredom. For those who are easily bored, prayer is an immediate necessity. Why? Satan preys upon the bored seeking to manipulate their boredom into work for his fiery kingdom. Therefore, fix your heart and mind immediately on the needs of and requests of others. Nearly simultaneously, you will find you have, by offering your own suffering, become detached from it and used it for the good grace of another soul.

"Stay faithful, my beautiful women, to the vocation to which you have also been called—wife, mother, single woman, but

always an ever-faithful prayer warrior. As you prepare for rest each evening, it is a necessity that you bind Satan in the name of my beloved Son, Jesus, over your dreams, over all your loved ones and claim your home as a house of prayer and a house of worship belonging to the children of God. In your dreams, God may reveal his plans for you. So, ask Jesus to prepare your heart to receive whatever it is that needs to be revealed to you.

"As you lift your eyes to the Lord, remember from whence your help always comes—it comes only from the Lord, the maker of Heaven and Earth. Make yourself a willing vessel of God's will with an ardent and unfailing desire to follow only His will for your life all the days of your life. Remember, the Lord our God, will keep you safe as you lie and sleep in peace.

"Be assured that I am with you now, praying with you and for you. My prayers for each of you will continue at the hour of your death and until your reunion with our beloved God in Paradise where I will greet you.

"I am Mary, Guardian of the Gates of Heaven and the Souls in Purgatory for whom I also always pray. May you also remember them always."

Scribed on July 24, 2021

About the Author

Irene Lynch is a former principal of Epiphany Cathedral School in Venice, Florida, and a member of the Catholic Writers Guild. She is a strong and passionate woman with an undeniable love for God, her husband, John, and her family. Her laugh is contagious, and her faith inspires many. Formerly from Massachusetts, she has been a Sarasota County, Florida resident since 1988. She is married to John Lynch and has three daughters: Jill Athridge, Jennifer McCarron, and Jackie McCallister, and three sons-in-law: Mark Athridge, Dave McCarron, and Doug McCallister. She graduated from Bourne High School in 1970 and Bridgewater State College (BSC) in 1974 with a Bachelor of Science in Elementary Education. She received her master's degree from the University of Southern Florida (USF) in Special Education and her EDS in Education Leadership from Nova Southeastern University. She taught kindergarten and first grade at Philippi Shores Elementary School, was a resource teacher and Exceptional Student Education (ESE) Liaison at Fruitville Elementary and was an assistant principal at Venice Middle and Sarasota Middle School before becoming Epiphany Cathedral School's principal. Irene is a passionate member of St. Patrick's Church and is involved with the Ladies Auxiliary of the Knights of Columbus, the Divine Mercy Cenacle, the Eucharistic Adoration team, the RCIA team, and the Bereavement team. She is a Eucharistic minister and was a member of the Legion of Mary at the Incarnation Church. Her community service included being a community director of the YMCA and delivering Meals on Wheels.

You can learn more at: Iftodayyouhearhisvoice.com